Keyworking in Social Care

Other SCA Co-publications

Residential Care: An International Reader
Meir Gottesman

The Children Act: A Social Care Guide
Ian Mallinson

Quality Counts: Achieving Quality in Social Care Services
Des Kelly and Bridget Warr (Editors)

Social Care: Rivers of Pain, Bridges of Hope
Leonard Davies

Yesterday's Answers:
Development and Decline of Schools for Young Offenders
Jim Hyland

Insights into Inspection:
The Regulation of Social Care
Roger Clough

Forthcoming:

Coping with Violence
Vaughan Bowie

Care Management and the New Social Work:
A Critical Analysis
Michael Sheppard

Social Care: An Introductory Reader
Des Kelly and Chris Payne

Managing Change in Social Care:
Des Kelly and John Harris

A Whiting & Birch Ltd / SCA (Education) Co-Publication

Keyworking in Social Care
A Structured Approach to Provision

Ian Mallinson

Whiting and Birch Ltd

MCMXCV

Published by Whiting & Birch Ltd,
PO Box 872, , London SE23 3HL, England.
USA: Paul & Co, Publishers' Consortium Inc, PO Box 442, Concord, MA 01742.

British Library Cataloguing in Publication Data.
A CIP catalogue record is available from the British Library

ISBN 1 871177 06 5 (cased)
ISBN 1 871177 12 X (limp)

Printed in England by Antony Rowe, Chippenham

Contents

Section Three: Keyworking in Practice: Examples

Acknowledgements

The author would like to acknowledge the assistance of the Social Care Association/British Association of Social Workers working party on keyworking (Vic Citarella, Charlotte Lodge, Val McCartan, Yvonne Morland, and Paul Richards) in compiling this volume. The idea for the volume was a direct result of their discussions. Thanks are due to John Harris, and Des Kelly for supervising the research. Thanks also to Chris Payne for editorial advice. The chapter on matching uses work by Vic Citarella who has also been a particular inspiration for the project. Similarly the chapter on co-keyworking uses material by Errol Best to whom particular thanks should be given. Practice material from Trevor Atkins, Steve Eyre, Phil Garland, Bill Haddow, Suzanne Johnston, Pat Lomax, Trish McFadden, Brenda McKie, Brenda Metcalfe, Bernie Moir, Mark Mungavin, Eileen O'Keefe, Suzie Roche, and Bronwen Yale is gratefully acknowledged. The help of Kathleen Lane on aspects of the chapter on special education, and the use therein of concepts contained in *Group Care Practice with Children* by L Fulcher and F Ainsworth (Tavistock, 1985) is also gratefully recognised.

Preface

The concept of keyworking has been subject to considerable lack of clarity which has militated against coherent development. This book attempts to codify the diversity of the many differing ways that keyworker systems may be constructed in social care. A single coherent methodology is created in which practice in a variety of social care settings may be developed and clear principles established. The book is divided logically into three sections:

Section One: Background

Chapters one and two define keyworker systems, set out the development of the diversity of systems and the range and types of application involved. Some research findings are reviewed and issues for the development of keyworking are posed.

Section Two:
Organising and Implementing Keyworker Systems

Chapters three to seven seek to establish a coherent framework for keyworker systems and keyworking practice. Chapter three sets out how a systems approach that also considers structures and action will enable this. Chapters four to seven examine each of the differing aspects or subsystems that comprise a keyworker system (care planning, individualised care, teamworking and management). The dynamics of each of these is investigated and principles of practice established. A check list for the development of each area is included.

Chapters eight to ten examine particular aspects of keyworking. Matching and co-keyworking are important areas of application. An example of implementing a keyworker system is discussed.

Section Three: Keyworking in Practice: Examples

Chapters eleven to fifteen examine keyworking in several different areas of specialist application giving several practice examples and how particular issues may be enabled in different settings and with different service user groups.

Ian Mallinson
Edinburgh
1995

Section One:

Background

One

An introduction to keyworking

WHAT IS KEYWORKING?

Keyworking is a system for providing individualised social care through named persons. A keyworker is the person who has responsibility and accountability for the care of the service user. Keyworkers help and support service users in making decisions relating to their situation.

WHAT KEYWORKING INVOLVES

According to SCA (1991) keyworking embraces:

- mutual trust and respect;
- the social physical intellectual cultural emotional and spiritual aspects of the service user's development and wellbeing;
- creating a sense of purpose and change;
- partnership between the keyworker other service providers and those who are the users of their services;
- planning (utilising the abilities of individuals and groups in the arena of problem solving);

- the changing of social environments (including for example the challenging of racist, sexist and ageist attitudes and behaviours).

BACKGROUND

In 1976 the then Residential Care Association (now the Social Care Association (SCA) and the British Association of Social Workers (BASW) produced a joint report on co-operation between field and residential workers. The keyworker was to take primary responsibility for coordinating and planning care based upon a close relationship between the worker and the service user. The keyworker would be the most appropriate person to carry out the task, irrespective of the setting.

This approach built upon linkworker schemes that had existed particularly in services for children and families in the 1960s.

Issues that concerned early keyworker systems were spanning the boundaries between rigid sectors of responsibility, and creating relationships that enabled a proper continuum of care.

Since 1976 differing forms of keyworking, based upon the needs of different contexts, have evolved. In the 1980s these became an extremely broad spectrum of provision. The range was from keyworkers focusing upon intimate relationships in the direct process of caring to keyworkers as named individuals acting as co-ordinators of child abuse investigations.

The nature of provision has been subject to a great deal of change, particularly after the implementation of the 1990 NHS and Community Care Act. The demands of legislation and guidance, and the purchaser provider split in the new system for community care, has polarised the spectrum that used to meet the needs of the previous decade.

Keyworking in area teams as the purchaser wing of departments now exists as a form of allocation of work to a named individual who has coordinating responsibilities in multidisciplinary teams (e.g. in child abuse investigations). In some cases this may be combined with the role of care manager.

Keyworking in social care settings functions as the provider wing of arrangements for community care. It now focuses upon utilising relationships to monitor and assess situations in order to make decisions regarding planning and seeing through individualised care. This may be in relation to an overall care planning agreement with a care manager, or may be freestanding where a care manager is not involved. This book concerns keyworking in social care only.

Keyworking may thus be a means of meeting individual needs in a care setting. It may enable a personalised service in a residential, day, or domiciliary care. It may also be a means of creating a clear basis for decision-making when different parts of an organisation are involved e.g. the linkperson in a children's home, between them and an area team.

The nature and interpretation of the role of the keyworker has clearly been subject to considerable shifts in definition, scope, purpose and approach. There has not been a unified or analytic view of the concept and most of the writings on keyworker 'systems' have been based purely upon theory rather than on actual practice. This book now uses a recent research study into the nature of keyworking, conducted by the author at the University of Warwick. It attempts to unify the various approaches in social care and provide a platform for the development of practice.

RESEARCH INTO THE NATURE OF KEYWORKING

The complex nature of keyworking practice is illustrated by some of the findings of that research project.

An aspect of the research was a postal survey of residential establishments for older people in a defined geographical area. Whilst caution should be exercised in applying the findings beyond the particular area and service user group, keyworkers as named persons had a particular a responsibility and accountability for planning and delivering individualised care in a large proportion of establishments. Of the 102 questionnaires returned, keyworkers occurred in 95% of statutory sector establishments. In the private sector incidence was 32%. Size of establishment appears to have been a factor here. Questionnaires returned indicated that keyworking enables staff and service users to make sense of the tension between individual care and group living. It can provide a focus for supervision, care planning, decision-making, and for quality control.

Keyworkers often appeared to exist as part of a wider infrastructure of care. Documents such as policy statements and charters of rights were found more frequently in establishments that had keyworkers than those without.

There were clear differences in individual care planing between establishments with keyworkers and those that did not have them (83% of establishments with keyworkers had two or more of items such as; review meetings, contracts/ agreements shared decision-making, action planning or mutual goal setting, as opposed to 52% in establishments without keyworkers).

The incidence of decision-making involving service users (via user's committees, staff/users meetings, reviews and informal day to day provision) was higher in establishments with keyworkers. 95% of keyworker systems had two or more forums for decision-making compared with 60% in establishments without keyworkers. Thus keyworking may be seen as part of a wider network of care practice.

Care planning was achieved through supervision at the different levels of day to day events, individual goal setting and planning for the setting. 93% of keyworkers were supervised (47% had individual supervision, and 60% group supervision). A problem solving approach was used in supervision in 54% of cases and a review of responsibilities in 53%. Only 25% of establishments used written agreements to supervise keyworkers. A greater prevalence of supervision occurred in large establishments. In the statutory sector all establishments with keyworkers had supervision.

It was found that 97% of establishments with keyworker systems felt that keyworking improved *personalised care*, 2% felt otherwise. According to respondents, keyworking enables:

- staff and service users to get to know each other;
- the fulfilment of service user's personal needs;
- self-esteem and dignity/ choice;
- individualised care on a one to one basis reflecting service user choice and trust;
- monitoring and reporting of any deterioration in the general wellbeing of the service user;
- job satisfaction and accountability.

Of establishments, 81% felt that keyworkers improved *relationships,* 2% felt otherwise. According to respondents, keyworking enables:

- getting to know each other;
- enhancement of trust;
- better communication;
- delegation;
- development of friendships with relatives.

Of establishments, 69% felt that keyworker systems improved the *clarity of the residential task* (10% felt that they did not). According to respondents, keyworking enables:

- a greater knowledge of the needs of the individual;
- fulfilment of aims and objectives;
- decisions supporting, resolving and planning;
- roles to be clarified;
- accountability;
- staff and service users to take pride in their own work.

Of establishments, 61% felt that keyworker systems improved other *aspects of the life of the establishment* (9% felt that they did not). Factors here appear to be:

- a more relaxed atmosphere and job satisfaction via good relationships and networks;

- attention to small but important matters, e.g. buying clothes, toiletries, cigarettes, letters, going on outings;
- decision-making via advocacy or counselling;
- flexibility, recognition, responsibility and management;
- identity and involvement with a member of staff strengthened;
- healthy competition between staff to better their service;
- meeting the needs of ethnic minority elders.

Some *problem areas* were however highlighted:

- resourcing difficulties e.g. a shortage of staff (sickness and annual leave) could result in a system breakdown;
- close monitoring needed to check that service user and staff are happy with their workload and are compatible;
- keyworkers leaving;
- part time staff may have difficulty building up relationships;
- individual service user rights lost in the system;
- constraints of level of commitment and shift system.

FURTHER DEVELOPMENT OF THE CONCEPT OF KEYWORKING

The results of this research and the SCA document (1991) all suggest that in keyworker systems the three areas of supervision, care planning and relationships in daily living may be seen to be dynamically related. The activities of the manager in assisting the keyworker in planning and the keyworker in linking care planning and relationships are dimensions of this. Keyworking may thus permeate all the 'layers' of the setting, and within a group. Thus the nature of the setting may be focused into individual requirements and in turn individual requirements enabled within the setting and/or group. Personalised relationships may be made more meaningful within a group as keyworking is used to enable individual needs.

In the next chapter it is found that only recently have keyworker 'systems' actually been viewed in this manner as a whole, or indeed as systems. Almost invariably these works have located keyworkers within a wider system. There thus appears to be no keyworker *systems* and of central concern must be the lack of a coherent framework in which to generate an understanding through which to resolve the many dilemmas and contradictions of practice that may be found.

It is clear from the research that the nature of keyworker practice is broader than the narrow base of past documentation. In this book a number of principles are developed for different forms of keyworking within an overall structure.

A framework is thus generated to provide explanations of social care practice and to provide a basis for considering practice wisdom systematically. Whether keyworking is a system or a sub-system of a wider whole, such a framework enables a composite and full view to be taken of the requirements that are needed in practice as a whole for keyworkers to function efficiently and effectively.

Following SCA/BASW (1987) a firm rationale for development of the concept is created, as the advantages of keyworking are said to clearly outweigh the disadvantages. They suggest that enabling factors (such as clear philosophies of care, supervision, support and training, teamwork and communication) can be further developed in all keyworking contexts so that their potential for system maintenance and development may be harnessed.

Keyworker systems may now be devised, and developed to meet the differing needs of the new contexts demanded in the late 1990s. The existing conceptualisation of keyworking is diffuse, and riddled with contradictions and tensions. These have mitigated against the development of coherent practice. The nativity of the 1970s and the pragmatism of the 1980s (explored in the next chapter) need re-translating in the 1990s into a new analytic framework in which clear principles can be located. The framework will be charged with providing the means to create models for particular individual practice contexts so as to enable the delivery of an effective and efficient standard of care.

Chapters three to seven of the book explore the issues that such a composite theory base will need and examine the interconnectedness of component parts and the process of caring. The meaning of interactions, roles and processes of activities contained within parts of keyworker systems are explored. Particular examples of practice within this framework are given in later chapters.

Before that composite framework is discussed, it is useful to first examine how the concept has developed. The historical diversity of interpretation and application all has a bearing upon the nature of current practice. In order to understand and work with the future it is essential to first understand the past. The next chapter therefore examines aspects of the development of keyworking.

Two

The development of keyworking

INTRODUCTION

The development of the keyworker concept can be seen to follow a number of broad, often overlapping phases. Several trends have merged, overlapped or continued in existence over time. The diversity of current practice reflects the diffuse and often undefined nature of all these developments. These approaches often still exist in different forms or combinations. It is useful to explore these so that an understanding of the nature of current practice may be obtained. It is only by considering the past, and the nature of present practice, that a platform may be created for keyworker systems to be developed further in the future.

EARLY HISTORICAL DEVELOPMENTS

The roots of the keyworker concept are to be found in the late 1960s and early 1970s in specialising and link roles in residential and day care particularly within children's services. Younghusband (1978) states that a pattern in residential care for children 'emerged by degrees (which) made caseworkers (in residential settings) responsible for particular residents and their families -often before admission - in co-operation with resident staff as well as for after care ... But there was continuing confusion about the respective roles and responsibilities of field and residential workers for residents and their families.' Link roles were founded in the pragmatism of individual settings.

The separation of roles and sectors within organisations were part of the dominant mechanistic bureaucratic cultures of the time (see for example Burns and Stalker, 1966). This was highlighted by the Seebohm Report (1968). Organisationally rigid boundaries existed between local authority divisions (fieldwork, residential care and domiciliary services) as well as between departments responsible for different service user groups. Berry (1975) in her research, illustrates practice in residential care that was isolated from fieldwork and children in turn isolated from local communities. Thus link roles may be seen as innovatory in relation to the dominant ideology, values and theoretical principles that applied at the time.

In this context, one of the emerging issues of the early mid 1970s was that residential work is part of social work (CCETSW, 1973; Harris, 1975). This as a general declaration espoused throughout most of the social services world promoted an re- examination of the boundaries between fieldwork and residential care.

In 1976, in the wake of these issues, the then Residential Care Association (now Social Care Association) and the British Association of Social Workers together sought to bridge the perceived gulf between practice in fieldwork and in residential work through individualised service user - worker relationships in which the 'keyworker' would be 'the person having full responsibility for the service user received into residential care and for decisions relating to the case.' (RCA/BASW, 1976). RCA and BASW sought to improve standards of practice particularly in relation to the continuity of experience for service users on admission to, and discharge from, residential care. The principles of accountability in decision-making, cooperative approaches and a unified service were promoted within the document.

Practitioners and managers proceeded to implement practice after the publication of the BASW/RCA report. Davis (1978) however highlights the organisational problems and constraints that had become significant given the ambiguities contained in the BASW/RCA recommendations. He specifically mentions 'the shadow of accountability... (and) ...divided loyalties' in the context of confidentiality, communication, and power in/ the power of relationships. Davis identifies the structural problem of an employee who is expected to be accountable to both service user and manager. He notes with concern that the keyworker may be incorporated into a 'spurious consensus' with other professional colleagues at the expense of the weakest party - the service user. Davis however quoted situations where keyworkers had developed relationships with service users of such quality that they became 'totally available and involved as advocates for service user's rights and champions in individualised development.'

Davis in reality posed the basic problem of social work/ social care that organisational climate and culture in many cases acts as a fundamental barrier to change. Personal experience of the author highlights that many organisations saw the development of keyworking, at this time, as a goal - directed approach rather than an issue concerning the process of change in the sense of organisational involvement. Such a process would have been more productive, instead change became an insurmountable problem.

The RCA/BASW document appears to tackle practical issues within a psychological base (residential and fieldwork staff should work together) and ignore the power and value dimensions of entrenched cultural and organisational rigidities, and the threats to individual workers and groups that these posed. Davis (1978) thus highlighted that a keyworker can only be as good as other workers and the system will allow.

The extreme role ambiguity of keyworking (i.e. what is

appropriate for the keyworker to do and where the boundaries exist) has been a recurrent theme. It is of significance in the realism that followed the implementation of the BASW/RCA report (1976) that most of the subsequent literature (particularly Burningham, 1983; Hogan, 1988; RCA, 1984; Meteyard, c.1986) focused upon keyworking as 'internal' to residential institutions. According to Wendelken (1983) the title 'specials' became interchangeable with that of keyworker.

In BASW (1985) and research by Challis and Davies (1986) keyworking also became a form of allocation to fieldworkers within their traditional role as primary (or often only) decision-maker in a service user's life. In practice much of the ideal of boundary spanning was lost. In this realism keyworking was reduced to a form of internal case allocation within (or outside) institutions.

Ward (1978) specifically discussed here the underplaying of the ideal of a keyworker as the person who was responsible for the 'progress through' (pre-admission, admission, and later, discharge and after care) of a service user in relation to the residential experience. She highlights the keyworker as the person responsible for 'deciding, and implementing a programme of care plus goal - directed activity specific to each resident'. The principle of planning and progressing/ coordinating care was clearly stated.

These developmental papers oscillate between idealism/ endeavours to exert change and realism. Much of the resulting practice may not (for a variety of reasons) actually meet the challenge of the ideals that were originally formulated.

In view of the central theme, concerning roles and crossing boundaries between sectors, it is useful to pause and examine this.

ROLES AND BOUNDARIES

The RCA/BASW historical view of the keyworker role and the need for boundary spanning gained academic credibility in Bromley's article in the *British Journal of Social Work*

(1977). Here was formulated the notion of case - accountable staff based upon reciprocal interaction between the two separate management hierarchies (residential and fieldwork). The 'prime care agent' would be responsible for enabling key decisions, for example, entry to residential care to be taken 'with precision'. Development was seen in terms of role definition on the one hand and delineation of tasks and activities with agreed areas of individual responsibility on the other. It was maintained that 'clarity of respective tasks would only set the boundaries within which negotiation and discussion could occur' although the 'quality of interaction' was felt to be the most significant factor in likely effectiveness. Elliott (1980) pursued these questions, analysing the high degree of overlap between the skills required of residential workers and field social workers, placing keyworking firmly within the residential task.

Meanwhile, Sackville (1979) placed the idea of keyworking as a boundary spanning activity in the historical development of the polarisation of residential work and field social work. The devaluation of residential work in research findings (e.g. Bowlby, 1963; Townsend, 1962) had been particularly significant here. For Sackville the rationale of the role lay in relationship building in institutions and in care planning, as well as changing the nature of role segregation. Sackville stated firmly the lack of clarity in the concept and of clear organisational patterns.

It is indicative of a service in 1979 still coming to grips with tensions within the keyworker concept, that three years after the BASW/RCA report, Rodway (1979) raised the question of to whom the keyworker was accountable (supervisor, team, or division) and how shared care would be organised. Questions of accountability (is a keyworker more or less accountable than staff in other roles?) and power (how does the keyworker relationship help (if at all) to resolve power issues?) were not addressed at the time. It is probable that the naivete of a lack of an overall perspective was one of the reasons why formal roles concerning boundary spanning never really materialised.

There is a virtual absence of reported cases that may be said to have had any degree of success in boundary spanning. White (1979) appears to have had some results from some very forceful individual negotiation from within a voluntary sector project. This may however be compared with other appraisals:

> Despite these attempts to implement new ideas such (keyworker) projects are in a minority and many departments still work on the prescriptive model of interaction between field and residential workers (Elliott, 1980).

> Although... (keyworking) ...is manifestly a good idea, the feasibility and advantages of such a method have never been properly tested (Davies, 1985).

Elkan and Kelly (1991) state that from the point of view of the service user of an establishment:

> ...the failure in practice to carry through the original concept of keyworking as bridging the field/residential worker divide can be seen as a reduction to the continuity of experience between 'the community' and the residential establishment.

The debates of the 1970s were largely located in a pragmatism that examined 'who does what?' and 'how?' within a nebulous idealism. Not surprisingly therefore by the early 1980s keyworking had lost its impetus. Simple and naive initial idealism (field workers and residential care staff need to work together) had been lost in practical problems and power differentials. Douglas and Payne (1980) focused on key issues such as: Who is accountable? Who is able to make decisions? How do we resolve disagreements? How can we generate trust and confidence? Asking the question 'What happened to the keyworker idea?' was founded in the low status of residential work and the lack of common vision and language. A systematic appraisal of roles and tasks had not been undertaken by departments and the term 'keyworker' was generally used in confusion because of the inherent weaknesses in its formula. Keyworking, Douglas and Payne suggested, 'tends to ossify roles and relationships'.

Even where the focus of keyworking had not concerned boundary spanning, the problem of balancing individual and collective interests was not addressed. The allocation of an individual keyworker implies individualised systems of care, yet users and keyworkers 'are part of a wider group within residential establishments' (Elkan and Kelly, 1991). Thus part of the ossification of roles and relationships concerned the tension of balancing individual choice against the interests of the wider residential community.

With hindsight perhaps some of the original expectations were unrealistic, if not theoretically unsound. Keyworking based upon the original RCA/BASW model of 1976 is now largely an unworkable historical phenomena. There has since been no unifying view of the concept.

Many writers such as Douglas and Payne (1980) endeavoured to resolve the contradictory nature of keyworking, by going back to basic role definitions. They tried to identify how keyworker roles may differ from those of others. They suggested that there could exist a variety of approaches based on differing objectives. Tailor - made role definitions could be formulated to meet differing needs.

Many works now examine keyworking purely in relation to 'internal' residential social work. These may acknowledge a degree of ambiguity yet express comprehensive ranges of roles concerning personal care and care planning. Hogan (1988) suggests that in residential care, residents and keyworkers should be 'matched' according to the task in hand based upon an analysis of the proposed role. Douglas and Payne (1987) suggest 'each (residential or day care) unit tends to develop its own prescription of duties for its keyworkers'.

DEVELOPMENT OF KEYWORKING IN RESIDENTIAL CARE: PRINCIPLES

Despite these problems, keyworking had become a meaningful idea as a specialising role within residential care. Principles of practice for the particular settings involved were developed. A DHSS study (1979) found that where each staff member had a special responsibility for a group of service users, there was evidence that they knew the users better and that pressure on staff was less (see Lishman, 1982).

Individualisation of personalised care by keyworkers was now recognised. A platform was created for an internal coordinating role. These provided ways of involving service users in decision-making and care planning.

Foe example, Burningham (1983) explored relationships between keyworkers and service users in relation to decision - making. Clear benefits to service users are indicated here, in terms of companionship, and 'doing things together'. Fulcher and Ainsworth (1985) describe keyworker responsibilities in group care for children, where a direct care worker co-ordinates all aspects of care and treatment for a particular child. 'The primary task of a keyworker is to be a special person in the eyes of the child and to be responsible for liaison with others on behalf of that child. As the person who has (the) most information about the child and his situation, she/he will be responsible for overall plans and will need to have authority to make decisions.' Activities carried out by the keyworker '...might include planning care and treatment...report writing, liaison concerning job finding or school attendance, formal counselling sessions, working with the family and so on'. The authors suggest that an action plan should describe how the keyworker would carry out these tasks and the plan should be incorporated as a formal feature of the service.

Tossell and Webb (1986) talk about:

> ...developing a special trusting relationship that ensures that the child benefits from a warm concern that encourages confidential communication of needs and assists the child to develop the confidence to take an interest in a determine his future.

They discuss keyworkers linking with field social workers and parents/ potential foster parents. Meteyard (c.1986) suggests how roles may be negotiated within settings. Personalised care and organisational issues are explored.

Fletcher (1985) showed how principles can be developed in an individual residential setting to guide 'internal' keyworking. The administrative arrangements in the staff team are stated together with the processes involved (e.g. on admission). Key issues are said to be staff support and group and individual supervision so that a framework exists to tackle issues such as the service user's social, emotional and physical health. Individualisation of care by keyworkers is said to be beneficial as it avoids regimented treatment and enables the special needs of service users to be worked with.

In Taylor (1985) keyworkers had a primary role in a particular establishment for the delivery of care; each keyworker was responsible for service users within a group living arrangement. Similarly Howe (1990) suggests that 'linkworkers' take personal responsibility for the care of one particular child and play a key role in the assessment and management of risk. Here creativity and flexibility appear to be the way that responsibility is devolved. SCA (1991) also suggest that keyworkers should be meeting the defined needs of Black children being looked after within residential care.

Previous work by the author (Mallinson, 1987a, 1989a, 1989c, 1989d) set out a set of principles for keyworking in residential care: operational guidelines for managerial practice (1987a) supervising keyworkers (1989c) promoting efficient working (1989b) and care planning (1989a). The basis of these works is to take keyworking as an overall framework for the delivery of personalised and individualised residential care and then to set out the principles for each area that are indicated by mainstream practice translated into a keyworking context. The devising and implementation of keyworking using this methodology (with particular reference to the management of change and to supervision) is given in Johnson (1988).

Mallinson and Citarella (1990) further developed this approach of defining and debating principles of practice in their discussion of matching keyworkers and service users. Here the factors of gender and race are particularly explored in relation to feelings and emotions of service users and ways of proceeding in the process of matching outlined.

In accumulating practice wisdom, it has been possible to establish clear principles to guide practice in keyworker systems in residential care. This is perhaps why the evidence in the Wagner report (NISW, 1988) had '...a great many favourable references to the keyworker concept'. It was seen by some as '...the most significant development in residential care for all client groups' and in another setting its 'promising development owed as much to improving the work satisfaction and contribution of staff as it does to ensuring that resident's needs are met effectively'. The confusion over the exact meaning of the term was, however firmly mentioned in the evidence.

Meanwhile SCA/BASW in an unpublished report of a working group (1987) firmly suggest that the keyworker in group care is usually seen as the person who is responsible for the individual care of service users based upon personalised relationships within the context of the group setting. The planning necessary to meet the needs of individuals and groups of service users may be carried out jointly between keyworkers and supervisors. The original banner goal of boundary spanning is here replaced with a practice reality of a proliferation of narrower roles and relationships.

Elkan and Kelly (1991) however summarise the approaches of keyworking in relation to group care as 'essentially individualised responses to the provision of care services'. They draw attention to Lee and Pithers (1980) who point out the problems associated with 'effectively detaching the individual from the social' and also Baldwin (1990) who states, 'we must beware of perpetuating services which plan their interventions solely on the individual level'. They draw attention to the integration of service delivery which is said by Hambleton and Hoggett (1990) to be an important development with clear messages for residential settings.

The tensions that exist between individual and group care are mentioned but not entirely resolved in any of the above literature concerning principles. Endeavours to resolve this issue are largely based upon the use of a systems approach which is a major theme later in this book.

DIFFUSION AND RECOGNITION: KEYWORKING IN OTHER SETTINGS

The development of these and similar principles of working laid the foundations for effective keyworking in different contexts. The proliferation of differing settings for keyworking within the continuum of care came onto the Barclay committee's agenda. The report (NISW, 1982) in considering the working basis of the continuum of care, argued for the development of keyworker roles and tasks based upon blurring of traditional boundaries between residential and fieldwork settings. This change of emphasis was from boundary spanning *roles* to boundary spanning *activities and relationships*. It became part of a broad thrust that opened the way for other arenas of welfare (i.e. ones without a focus on residential/ fieldwork inter-relationship) to see keyworking as a means of developing clarity in care planning. This clarity could be achieved whilst still focusing decision - making within the service user/ worker relationship.

It is this spectrum of keyworker roles, in different settings, each developing their own tasks and activities that begins to form a sound basis for a stable theory of keyworking. That theme is one of the reasons for this book. The tensions of role conflict and boundary spanning have not been resolved, rather they have been moved aside and no longer appear insurmountable or necessarily even relevant. The idea of the keyworker as care planner is one which has developed considerably from these approaches. The extra dimension that is given by keyworking is one of co-ordination in the context of personalised relationships.

A number of examples of utilising keyworkers in different contexts now exist. Some of these are described below.

Dubois, Mockler and Mockler (1984) explored the flexibility resulting from re-defining roles between social workers and short term foster parents. The purpose of this was to prepare for transition. In designating the foster parents as keyworkers, their responsibilities were based upon therapeutic working through of the child's emotional preparedness for the transition. Roles here had to be clearly defined. The flexibility of working across traditional boundaries appears, according to the authors, to have been beneficial.

Riordan, Bramhall and Backhouse (1988) explore keyworking in the community with elderly persons. Here matching skills and relationships, the process of care planning and role accountability were issues that had to be addressed. These themes are also stated in Gray and Isaacs (1979). Similar attempts to resolve the lack of role clarity in meeting the community needs of chronically disabled elderly persons was raised by Challis, Darton, Johnson and Stone (1988). The issue of co-ordination and avoidance of overlap was resolved by redefinition of roles and boundaries. 'Multi-purpose keyworkers' were created. This project (The Darlington Community Care Project) was said to exist in sharp contrast to boundary disputes (regarding tasks and responsibilities) and conflicts of interests (generated by differential service aims and agendas) itemised by Savage (1985).

The Social Services Inspectorate (1989) gave unqualified approval to keyworking as a means of co-ordination in the establishment of local procedures for multidisciplinary assessment of the needs of elderly people:

> Multi-disciplinary assessment is likely to increase the numbers of elderly people whose wish to stay in their own home can be realised through the provision of individualised packages of care...Responsibility for the co-ordination of these inputs should be vested in a nominated keyworker...to ensure that the client's wishes are sought and reflected in the overall package of services offered and so that adjustments to individual

components are made known to other services involved, who may in turn need to be modified.

The overall nature of keyworking was seen as a means of creating organisational frameworks for new systems of community care. Keyworking gave the means to resolve problems arising from organisational boundaries and rigid occupational roles. As an approach to decentralisation, keyworking was said to provide the possible answer to problems of budgetary control in care management and to devising and coordinating responsive care packages. (Challis, 1985). This theme is further developed later in this chapter.

Research by Glendinning (1986) considers 'single door approaches' in social work with families of disabled children. A new specialist role was based upon needs expressed in consumer research. Keyworkers were given a brief to change any role preconceptions creatively and to deal with the whole spectrum of problems that presented themselves. The resulting range of advice and information (concerning disability, handicap, medical health care, education, residential care, recreation and leisure, practical problems of daily care, housing problems, adaptations and equipment for the home, family finances, emotional and family problems, access to resources etc.) transcended professional boundaries. A keyworker's relationship here was as a kind of friend. It contrasted with the formal co-ordination role of keyworkers in multi-disciplinary teams.

Renshaw et al. (1988) surveyed 28 pilot projects designed to move long stay patients out of hospital funded under the Government's Care in the Community initiative. Of these several used keyworkers in co-ordination, liaison and continuity of care. There were many different authorities, settings and approaches involved. For example:

- Bolton moved people with learning difficulties to adapted housing with staffing support, sheltered accommodation and family placements. Named keyworkers were coordinators of individual care plans.
- Calderdale used keyworkers for generating assessments.

- Warrington had a number of keyworkers each fully responsible for four service users with mental illness.
- Coventry in placing elderly persons had keyworkers working with a multi-disciplinary admissions panel.
- Hillingdon, in working with elderly mentally infirm persons had keyworkers responsible for progressing care plans prepared by a multi-disciplinary team.

Keyworkers in some instances were of professional groups other than social workers. The clear message in this survey is the diversity of roles, tasks and management structures that were involved across the country. For example, assessment and planning ranged from collation of information on paper, to formal meetings convened by keyworkers. Working situations ranged from relative isolation, to effective use of individual supervision and team support. The amount of contact with service users by keyworkers varied enormously, depending upon the priority attached to relationships or co-ordination. Keyworking was said by the research group to be the most effective means of assessing the needs of service users on an individualised basis. It was also most effective in progressing and implementing individual planning (based upon the exercise of judgment, imagination and experience).

These developments focus upon keyworkers in co-ordinating roles resolving some of the problems of multi-disciplinary work. This contrasts with the primary emphasis upon relationships that is to be found in residential care.

Keyworking in multi-disciplinary teamwork with mental handicapped people is said to illustrate the benefits of the single door, provision of a care package, extra advice and ready access by service users. Ferlie, Pahl and Quine (1984) show that keyworking promotes effectiveness here. Issues such as keyworker 'power' within the team, interpretation of role, and service user orientation in referral policies, need to be addressed. Greater parental involvement was promoted by the appointment of keyworkers with a wide and comprehensive interpretation of their role. Boundaries between roles, within the team and outside, were issues to be resolved. Woolrych (1987) and Cotmore, Sinclair, Webb and Wistow (1985) again echo these points, Woolrych raising also issues of accountability and co-ordination.

Plank (1982) found that 71% of Community Mental Handicapped Teams (CHMT) always assigned a keyworker to families and 12% sometimes assigned a keyworker. Keyworkers were used to provide a contact point for parents and to ensure follow-up of treatment plans. A greater involvement of keyworkers in CHMTs who work on a day to day basis was found, than District Health Teams (DHT) who were more involved in assessment and co-ordination. (The results for DHTs were 42% always making assignments and 21% sometimes making assignments.)

To Anderson (1982) keyworking is the 'ideal' method of operation in Community Mental Handicap Teams so that a structure is given to each service user. As a preferred means of ensuring fail-safe contact and responsibility, effectiveness is said to hinge upon co-operation. Similarly research by Quine and Pahl (1989) in considering support to families states that each handicapped child should have a named person, 'who would be responsible for carrying out a *regular* assessment of his or her needs and for liaising with other professionals in order to provide the best service package for each family...' In Anderson's overall appraisal of the literature, different team approaches, and the question of boundaries and role within and outside the team, appear to remain central to keyworking in multidisciplinary work.

Beardshaw and Towell (1990) in relation to case management raise flaws to be addressed in keyworking within multi-disciplinary work:

> ...inter-professional rivalries can compromise effective working;...interpretations...may be coloured by particular professional backgrounds, with the result that clients receive a markedly different service depending on the keyworker they have been assigned. This problem can be exacerbated by a tendency to

> define the role very widely and ascribe a multitude of tasks to it. As a result...individuals...develop their own - limited - interpretations of what being a keyworker involves...

These issues had been acknowledged in contributions by Grant, Humphreys and McGrath (1986) and strategies to address them were being developed.

SCA/BASW (1987) examined 'illustrations of present practice'. These were: keyworkers in a home for elderly people, community mental handicap teams, child in care and child abuse. The approach was to identify four of the most common, or differing systems, and examine their dimensions so that a comparisons could be made. An summary of these four ideal types based upon SCA/BASW (1987) is presented in the following diagram (pp.28-29).

Keyworker systems within social care settings address the purposes of care planning and the individualisation of care based upon continuing relationships. Keyworking within child abuse teams and community mental handicapped teams enable clarity of responsibility and decision - making in care planning processes and the co-ordination of multidisciplinary roles. Keyworking for children in care is probably the nearest model to that of the RCA/BASW document of 1976 but has moved away from much of the purity in boundary spanning of the original and acknowledges many of the problem issues involved.

FORMALISATION: KEYWORKER SYSTEMS

Virtually all the literature states the existence of keyworker systems, yet in most cases there is little examination, if any, of the nature actual systems. Elliot (1978) first set up an overall systemic model that contains keyworking as an essential ingredient. Elliot attempted to express systems and sub-systems based upon an 'integrated model' located from residential establishments. In common with the early systemic approaches in social work, it fails to address the dilemmas and power relationships of everyday practice. By omission it contradicts current (changed) thinking concerning the need for feedback within systems in social work (Ross and Bilston, 1989; Douglas and Payne, 1988).

In a working paper, RCA (1984) proposed the need for a holistic appraisal of the effect of keyworker systems upon residential establishments, in particular upon staff themselves and upon issues in group living. RCA presented the view that keyworking demanded new ways of working throughout establishments in terms of democratic management styles, team management rather than bureaucratic control, avoidance of hierarchical accountability and in the use of life space:

> The role of keyworker is shaped, not only by the perceptions of the keyworker but by the expectations of others... (keyworking) ...moves boundaries, therefore leads to other roles in the system being re-appraised and re-defined. The total role-set is itself created and sustained by those who establish their positions within it...The tendency appears to have been to focus on *job enrichment* rather than job enlargement...practices can be...sustained in establishments in such a way as to both further the social treatment of residents/clients and to enlarge and enrich the work of care staff.

Following earlier work by the DHSS (1976) which instructed social services departments that one of the participants at child abuse case conferences should be nominated as keyworker, BASW (1985) located keyworking roles within carefully defined systems for managing child abuse. The DHSS had earlier defined the role (1976) as:

> The professional most closely concerned with the case and responsible for its actual management...identified as the focal point through whom information is channelled and is made responsible for ensuring it reaches all other participants.

Social work and case conference practice arising out of this

Illustrations of Keyworker Practice
Analysis of the report of the joint SCA/BASW working group 1986 *Review and Prospect: 10 Years of Keyworking*

Dimension	Home for Elderly People	Community Mental Handicap Teams	Child in Care	Child Abuse
Function	Group care, Quality of life	Normalisation, Individualisation	Rehabilitation, Care in the Community	Child protection
Title	Keyworker (internal)	Named worker	Keyperson	Keyworker
Personnel involved	Care assistant	Instructor, ATC manager, Social worker, Community nurse, Residential worker, Psychologist, Psychiatrist	Residential SW, Teacher, Foster parent, Social care worker, Field social worker, Nursery worker	Social worker
Illustrative keyworker roles	Meeting needs, Tending needs (ie: physical, intellectual, emotional, social), Recording & reporting	Care planner, Carer, tending with advocacy advisor	Care planner, Therapist, Link supervisor/guardian, Befriender, Advisor, Case accountability	Officer of the court, Case management coordinator, Case accountability
Illustrative contacts for keyworkers	Relatives, District nurse	Instructor, ATC manager, Community nurse, Psychologist, Psychiatrist	School, Child guidance, B. agency parents	Police, Parents, GP, School, NSPCC, Nursery family centre
Illustrative tasks	Special relationships/Implementing/Counselling/Recording & reporting/Communicating PLUS:			
	Physical care, Enabling & facilitating, Behavioural management, Observation, Collecting & relaying information	Representing, Enabling & facilitating, Collecting & presenting information, Physical care, Behavioural management, Planning & coordinating	Developing & maintaining social skills, Reviewing, planning & coordinating physical care, Representing, enabling & facilitating, Collecting information & presentation, Behavioural management	Reviewing, Planning & coordinating, Developing & maintaining social skills, Enabling & facilitating, Collecting & presenting information, Representing

Keyworker records	Log sheets	IPP system, Log sheets	Assessment reports, Case file	Conference reports, Case file
Manager of keyworker	Officer in charge	Review coordinator	Team leader, Officer in charge	Area officer
Illustrative manager roles	Supervision, Case accountability, Training, Matching keyworker & user	Monitoring, Training, Service development, Matching keyworker & service user	Supervision (according to establishment philosophy), Matching keyworker & user	Monitoring (according to statutory & agency requirements)
Management process	Identification of needs, Care plan review	Assessment & IPP, Goal planning, Opportunity planning	Assessment, Treatment plan, Care agreement or contract, Statutory review	Investigation, Assessment conference, Action planning
BENEFITS OF PRACTICE				
To service users	Personalised service, Continuity of care, Regular review, Improved recording, Personal care plans	Personal care plans, Continuity of care, Improved inter-agency cooperation, Single access approach, Participation in decision-making	Personalised service, Continuity of care, Regular review, Improved recording, Personal care plans	Better protection, Treatment prevention of further abuse
To keyworkers	Improved job satisfaction and interest/Greater ability to cope with stress/Better understanding of users/Better communication networks/ Improved development opportunities PLUS:			
	Even distribution of work, Recognition, Financial enhancement	Even distribution of work, Recognition	Even distribution of work, Recognition, Financial enhancement	Greater access to resources, Pooling of knowledge & skills, Sharing of responsibility
To managers	Recruitment aid/Work load management PLUS:			
	Improved knowledge of users/ Better job satisfaction/Delegation/ Staff development/Use of resources			Accountability of workers
General	Positive environment, Clarity of purpose & objectives, Teamwork, Cost-effective, Early problem identification	Better public relations & access into the community, Cost-effective, Early problem identification	Positive environment, Clarity of purpose & objectives, Teamwork, Cost-effective, Early problem identification	Public accountability, Clarity of purpose

approach is refined into specific practice guidelines in Moore (1985) and DHSS (1988). Overall this now represents a process of *formalisation* whereby keyworking gives a means to provide named persons in statutory situations, with responsibility for tasks such as co-ordination in multi-disciplinary working.

Brent (1985) state the problems and confusion that emerged in situations where both a formal keyworker existed (for child abuse investigation) and a linkworking keyworker existed in a residential establishment. Cooper and Ball (1987) and Brent (1985) both illustrate some of the other issues that had to be addressed in getting the working of the child abuse system right. Here the problems of multi-disciplinary working with health visitors who were reluctant to take on coordinating roles forced the distinction between the keyworker who had statutory case management responsibilities and the prime worker who may undertake most of the work with the family. Cooper and Ball comment upon the sense of isolation felt when the keyworker was responsible for the whole operation of a case. In locating keyworkers as coordinators in a wider system rather than posing a keyworker system in its own right, a different mode of thinking was promoted analogous to further developments in case/ care management systems which I propose to examine next.

MANAGERIALISM OF KEYWORKING: CARE MANAGEMENT SYSTEMS

Specific systems approaches were defined for care management during the lead up to the implementation of the White Paper, *Care in the Community* (HMSO, 1989). The notion of care management (or as termed earlier in the debate case management) stems from practice in the USA and an ideologically derived view that efficiency should be promoted in British social service delivery.

The designation of keyworkers in care management is now to a certain extent a historical phenomena. The Government requirement that the purchaser provider split was to be paramount has rendered the boundary spanning of keyworkers a redundant concept. It is indicative however of the strength of feeling in the debates of the recent past that in a survey of projects, Ferlie, Challis and Davies (1989) projected keyworker roles as essential 'to pull services together'. Building upon keyworking in multi-disciplinary work, keyworking was said to form an essential element within the initial British case management experience, where efficiency has been a proven factor.

The linking of planning and personalised care into one coherent system was the rationale for basing care management on community keyworking. In the development of pilot projects keyworker systems were seen as central to addressing planning in the same context as issues such as decision-making focused within the service user relationship. This was in order to create forums for independence, and the respect of self determination and choice. Problems of role clarity were initially resolved through keyworking, as were the need for a single door approach linking of management/ planning and intimate caring practice.

Projects were overtaken by Government guidance suggesting that keyworkers as care managers would not normally have responsibility for service delivery (Department Of Health/Scottish Office, 1991). Thus the separation of purchaser provider roles is now seen as paramount. Early on, in pilot projects e.g. in Kent, keyworking was abandoned largely because of the classic problems that we outlined earlier in this chapter.

The use of the keyworker concept in pilot projects was confused. This is illustrated by comparing Hunter (1988) and research by Challis et al. (1989). Hunter (1988) reports that there were keyworkers who were sometimes referred to as case managers or coordinators and vice versa. He was then very specific about the ideal, stating that:

> Keyworkers in general have a much narrower role (than case managers) that is service - specific. Whereas a client may have several keyworkers if he or she

> passes through a range of different services, there will be only one case manager for each client...He or she is there to facilitate the co-ordination and efficient allocation of services.

Challis et al. (1989) are equally specific but different, in that the co-ordination of care 'by an individual keyworker' (who takes on the role of case manager) is carried out in the context of inter-professional collaboration.

Redding (1991) stated that 'the starting point of the keyworker... (as care manager, which was) ...the idea of one identified person responsible for care whom the client knows and who would open up access to the system', became untenable. It encapsulated the tension and split between provider and purchaser. The guidance states that in multi-disciplinary primary care teams, there will probably be a designated practitioner (from any agency or profession) coordinating the work with the user (DOH/SO, 1991a). Thus in some residual cases there may be a keyworker designation. The advantages to the user of this approach are said to be of unlimited access to expertise, clear accountability, and a holistic approach. There is however a risk of inter-agency collusion. Abuse of the professional role, by keyworkers acting within, rather than beyond their professional discipline or remit, is also possible.

PROVIDER SETTINGS

Government requirements in specific areas for community care (e.g. mental health: DOH, 1993, 1990) highlighted keyworkers in provider settings. Here roles as monitor of patient's circumstances in relation to care planning responsibilities carried out by other parties are outlined. Keyworkers utilised their intimate knowledge of the service user's needs gained from individualised primary caring relationships (as opposed to third party relationships coordinating the day to day contact of others).

Following Cambridge (1992) and Dant and Gearing (1990) keyworkers in provider settings assume some direct care support for individual service users. They enable service user's day to day needs to be monitored and support to be provided. The detailed knowledge of service users that is necessary for planning is gained through such daily contact. Keyworkers therefore (in addition to their direct caring role) need to liaise closely with decision-makers. They feed information directly into IPP or case reviews, or indirectly via other workers such as case/care managers.

This is an entirely different form of boundary spanning than that which historically operated in the 1970s. The context of the purchaser /provider split may now be encapsulated by suggesting that social work may be loosely seen as purchasing and social care as providing.

Keyworkers in social care provide ongoing implementation of care packages after the initial involvement of the care manager. They are able to provide continuity and progression. Keyworkers have the critical relationship and are able to develop a programme of change. They are able to empower the service user, helping them to describe their ongoing needs. They are a crucial part of provision for advocacy. The richness of setting goals and achieving them with the service user is the keyworker's task in social care.

CONCLUSIONS

This discussion on the historical development of keyworking indicates particular future needs. Developments in keyworking in social care (i.e. provider settings) will need to have:

- clearly focused yet interlinking systems;
- definition of roles that avoid conflict and have agreed expectations;
- a clarity in the scope, purpose and effect of boundary spanning;
- a focus upon the nature, and separation of (but also links between) relationship based keyworking and co-ordination roles;

- trust, reciprocation and teamwork between and within sectors;
- a distinction between intimate personal care and the cost efficient management of services;
- a continuum of provision in which continuity is the byword;
- firm and close liaison between decision-makers;
- clear ways in which service user needs are advocated.

These issues form part of a composite framework for practice, utilising systems theory, that is developed in subsequent chapters.

Section Two:

Organising and Implementing Keyworker Systems

Three

A systems approach to keyworking

INTRODUCTION: SYSTEMS, STRUCTURE AND ACTION

This chapter creates a framework for keyworking practice. The framework provides a means to develop practice in a coherent manner.

Following Giddens (1979) a fruitful way of looking at systems is to see them in relation to the structures they are part of and the action that takes place within them. Thus the nature of the system and its structural properties may be developed by an examination of the links between component parts. The subjective meaning of interactions, roles and processes for the persons involved should also be considered.

Concepts from management, social work and social science, in relation to the practice of keyworking, and its significance for service users, can be examined as a whole. Practice wisdom can be placed in the framework generating fresh insights. The structure is determined by the nature and effect of settings, and the culture to be found within them. Personal goals of the participants (service users, carers, managers, keyworkers and their colleagues) in the process of caring generate a cluster of activities. The significance of practice for all concerned forms part of the outcomes of settings.

In the context of the current quest for efficiency and effectiveness in social care, the framework may be used to work through a number of issues:

- inputs and outputs of settings;
- practice evaluation, focusing on achievement resulting from a variety of roles and actions; and
- examination of processes and unstructured problems that may be contained within the nature of the task.

These issues may be differently defined by the persons involved, from their different roles and personal perspectives.

The start of generating the framework is to 'map' out all the component parts of keyworking and the pattern of their inter-relationships.

A MAP OF KEYWORKING

Keyworking focuses on improving the *quality of life* for the service user. The application of ideas to achieve this aim are considered within four areas of practice these are considered in detail in the chapters that follow later in this section of the book:

- *Roles and relationships.*
- *Teamwork.*
- *Decision-Making.*
- *Management.*

These elements are considered as a whole at three different levels in the setting:

- *Everyday practice .*
- *Care planning .*
- *An overall view of the setting.*

This gives an integrated, multi- dimensional view of the task. Concepts have been placed within the resulting 'map' in their main location (see figure, p.39).

A MAP OF KEYWORKING

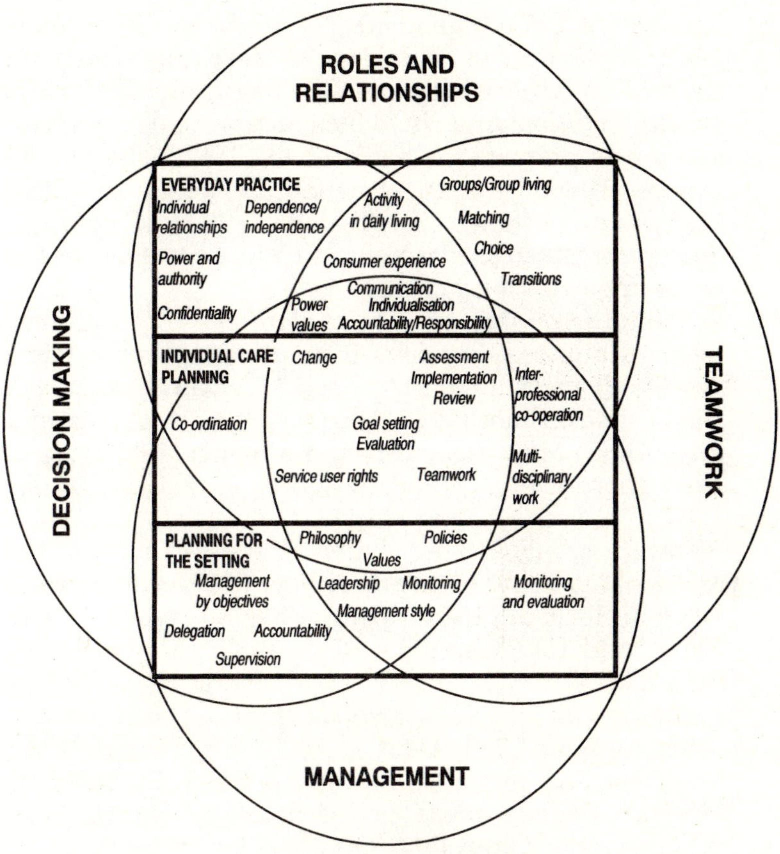

AIM: TO PROMOTE THE QUALITY OF LIFE OF SERVICEUSERS

CONCEPTS WITHIN KEYWORKING

A review was made of research and theoretical works concerning keyworker systems in relation to the map of keyworking practice. These findings are discussed in the chapters that follow. The main points are noted below:

- Achievement of a high *quality of life for service users* is assumed to be the main aim of keyworker systems. Central to keyworking practice are *individual user-worker relationships* in which accountable *decision-making* is promoted (Challis et al., 1988; Challis and Davies, 1986; Dant et al., 1989; Ferlie et al., 1984; Mallinson, 1989a; RCA/BASW, 1976). *Consumer experience* linked to *communication* and *power* appear to be an important part of this.
- *Roles* and *accountability* are joined in keyworker systems. Responsibilities of workers in relation to service users may be clearly stated (Bromley, 1977; Dant et al., 1989; Davis, 1978; Elliot, 1978; Hogan, 1988; Mallinson and Best, 1987; Mallinson, 1989a; Mallinson, 1989b; RCA, 1983; Riordan et al., 1988; Sackville, 1979; SCA/BASW, 1987).
- *Service users rights* in relation to the setting and the relationship figure highly (Bromley, 1977; Burningham, 1983; Ferlie et al., 1984; Hogan, 1988; Meteyard, c.1986; Payne and Douglas, 1983; RCA, 1983; Riordan, 1988; SCA/BASW, 1987).
- Principles such as *individualisation*, and choice (Burningham, 1983; Dant et al., 1989; Hogan, 1988; Mallinson and Best, 1989; Mallinson, 1989b; SCA/BASW, 1987) are linked to ideas such as *matching* (Hogan, 1988; Mallinson and Citarella, 1990).
- Settings may dictate particular requirements. Examples include *groupwork / group living*, *transitions*, *dependency and independence* (Burningham, 1983; Dubois and Mockler, 1984; Garland, 1987; Mallinson, 1989b; Meteyard, c.1986; SCA/BASW, 1987).
- Processes in keyworking have their own requirements.

For example, *care planning,* involves *assessment*, *goal-setting, decision-making, monitoring* and review (Challis and Davies, 1986; Dant et al., 1989; Mallinson, 1989a).

- The *outcomes* of a setting determine effectiveness. Aspects include *change*, and *avoiding institutionalisation* and *dependency* (Burningham, 1983; Dubois and Mockler, 1984; Mallinson, 1989b; Meteyard, c.1986).
- *Philosophy of care* largely determines the mission of the keyworker (Burningham, 1983; Dant et al., 1989; Elliot, 1978; Ferlie et al., 1984; Mallinson, 1987a; Meteyard, c.1986; Riordan et al., 1988; SCA/BASW, 1987).
- *Quality of life* is determined by action taken by the staff *team* within their particular *value base* (Burningham, 1983; Dant et al., 1989; Ferlie et al., 1984; Meteyard, c.1986; Riordan et al., 1988; SCA/BASW, 1987).
- *Teamwork* as a focus of keyworking involves co-ordination, and *multi-disciplinary working*, the extent of this will depend upon the nature of the setting (Challis et al., 1988; Ferlie et al., 1984; Riordan et al., 1988.
- *Leadership* of the team enables *accountability* based upon delegation (Mallinson, 1987a; Mallinson, 1989c; SCA/BASW, 1987). Clear policy *and planning*, and *supervision* of keyworkers promotes effectiveness.

A SYSTEM FOR ACTION

Keyworking may provide an integrated focus for conducting various elements of social care (e.g. care planning, management/supervision of staff, decision-making, monitoring and evaluation). A keyworker system will provide a reference point for carrying out a structured approach to provision. In moving beyond traditional approaches that purely emphasise the individual relationship aspects of keyworking, an integrated perspective is now considered.

The three most important areas (or sub-systems) of keyworker systems are care planning (see discussion to follow in chapter five), management (see chapter seven), and relationships in daily living (see chapter four). These should be considered in the context of teamwork (see chapter six). All these sub-systems are to be seen in a dynamic relationship. The activities of the manager in assisting the keyworker in planning, and the activities of the keyworker in progressing care planning within relationships, may also be represented as two axis linking these spheres of activity (see figure, p.43): Planning will occur at all levels: individual, group and setting. To be effective, it will be integrated with service user decision-making (on a day to day basis, as an individual planned approach, and in relation to policy and philosophies of the setting as a whole). Care planning is discussed in detail in chapter five.

Management and supervision are essential to the effective working of keyworkers. Management will enable the wider context of keyworking to focus on quality and enable the system to operate smoothly. Supervision will enable and support accountable practice. Management and supervision are discussed in detail in chapter seven.

Relationships are the life blood of keyworking. The provision of individualised care is maintained through relationships. These are discussed in detail in chapter four.

Teamwork sets the wider corporate notion of accountability and development. It provides a basis for continuity and support. Teamwork is discussed in detail in chapter six.

These sub systems of care planning, management of keyworkers, and relationships in daily living, contain elements that interlink at three levels of operation (across the setting, with the individual user/keyworker and in every day practice within the group/between individuals). These levels were discussed previously in connection with the map of keyworking (see figure p.39). The table overleaf (see p.44) sets out this structure.

The tone and ethos of each of the sub-systems may involve their own principles of practice that together promote a holistic approach. Following NISW (1988) and SSI (1989) core values such as privacy, dignity, independence, choice, rights and fulfilment are relevant. For example, relationships

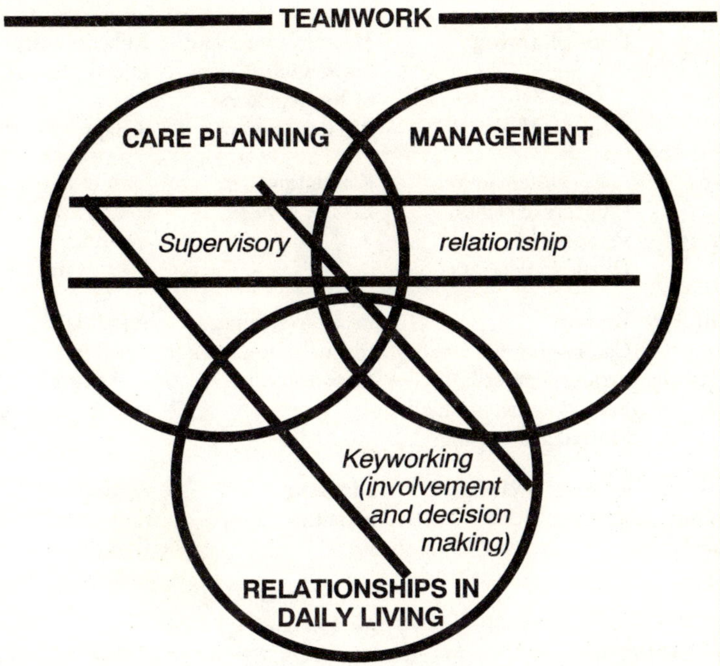

Axis for activity in relation to sub systems for planning, management, relationships and teamwork

in daily living may be promoted through principles involving individualisation within the group context. Care planning may be promoted through involvement and agreement, and management/supervision through consultation and reciprocation in relationships. All these activities focus upon service user(s) needs. Personalised relationships become more meaningful within the reference point of the group. Keyworking can enable individual needs whilst still focusing upon the overall dynamics and requirements of group living.

A systemic view of the structure of activities provides a basis for re-focusing keyworker systems, giving greater clarity. Sub systems can now be developed with their own principles of practice, and aims and objectives. Group and

Table

	Care planning (Chapter Five)	**Management and supervision of keyworkers** (Chapter Seven)	**Relationships in daily living**[1] (Chapter Four)
Across the setting	Policy statements; Charters of rights; Prospectus; Discussion documents.	Evaluation; Review of roles.	User/staff committees; Meetings of user groups.
With the individual	Reviews; Contractual arrangements; Shared decision-making; Mutual goal setting.	Problem solving; Review of keyworker responsibilities.	Allocation/ matching; Co-keyworking (providing cover).
In everyday practice	Informal decision-making.	Directing activities.	Setting up networks; Carrying out tasks.

1. *The relationship aspects of the keyworking task may be seen as linking everyday practice, and working across the setting as well as working with the individual.*

individual needs can be linked together. Overall a holistic philosophy can be created.

The interlinking of component parts can thus be enabled by design and meaningful connections made in practice. Decision-making and evaluation may take a wider view than previous narrow considerations that considered individual relationships linked into meeting needs. In group care, for example, keyworking will also provide a basis for relationships and planning permeating all the 'layers' of the setting, and within the group. Thus aspects of the group will emerge within individual requirements and in turn individual requirements will be enabled within the group. Personalised relationships are meaningful within a group identity because of the reference point of keyworking in enabling individual needs.

SUMMARY AND CONCLUSIONS

A systems view of the structure of keyworking activities in social care provides a basis for developing and focusing structures and action with greater clarity than hitherto. Systems and sub-systems can now be defined (in terms of aims and objectives and principles of practice) to carry out activities in the context of the whole. In creating a holistic philosophy, component parts of the task and activities to carry out the task can be deliberately interlinked and seen in a wider context. Meaningful connections may be made within the structure, and appropriate action enabled. Care planning, and activities such as decision-making and monitoring and evaluation may take a wider view than previous narrow considerations that merely just considered individual relationships.

These component parts are now examined in detail in the chapters that follow. Each sub-system together with the overarching concept of teamwork are taken in turn.

Four

Relationships in individualised care

INTRODUCTION

Relationships within keyworker systems will seek to:

- enable the exercise of personal choice by service users in all decision-making and in all aspects of daily living;
- promote openness between keyworkers and service users throughout all the process of social caring;
- promote honesty and reciprocal responsibility between keyworkers and service users based upon trust.

The wide variety of tasks that keyworkers undertake concerning individualised care are used as a medium to achieve these. These tasks include:

- acting as agent;
- devising and implementing care plans;
- counselling;
- recording and reporting;
- physical care;
- enabling developing, maintaining, and facilitating social skills;

- behavioural reviewing;
- coordinating;
- representing.

When carrying out these and other tasks, their nature may be discussed between the service user and the keyworker. As the process of individualised care is undertaken, personal choice in the decisions involved may be continually and openly discussed in partnership. This will cover all aspects of daily living. Honesty and trust may be established within the partnership between keyworkers and service users. Responsibility for the decisions may be shared and reciprocated.

THE AUTHORITY OF THE KEYWORKER

Authority for the keyworker to carry out their task is based upon its legitimation within the user, keyworker relationship. The outcomes of that relationship will depend upon what each of those involved allow to happen or tacitly agree may happen. This highlights the importance of an exchange and communication of feelings.

The role of keyworker will be determined by an agreed understanding of the meaning of the relationship. A primary factor here is the authority given by the user or their agent (as consumer/ contractor of the service). This allows the keyworker to interpret their role. A shared understanding will be beneficial to both parties and may be gained through reciprocal agreement.

THE CONTEXT OF THE KEYWORKER / SERVICE USER RELATIONSHIP

Relationships form a network of meaningful connections in the life of service users. This gives many possibilities for the way users' quality of life may be affected. Keyworkers will thus need to work with all members and components of the service user's experience. The keyworker may become the most significant part of that network in providing a clear point of identification for the service user in relation to the organisation or establishment. Following Raven and Rubin (1976) relationships that give a feeling of identification may be linked to feeling comfortable with a person, and feelings that they are prepared to make efforts on one's behalf.

Within group care it is important that the service user feels positive about group membership. The group should give an element of reassurance rather than be seen as a threat. As Douglas (1986) says 'liking is still a highly personal matter, though group membership can modify the individual perception of what is likable'. Douglas goes on to say that acceptance provides support and a tangible sense of security, warmth, and affection accompanied by self esteem. As a very significant member of the social network of the service user part of the keyworker's role is to make sure that acceptance is promoted within the group.

Creating relationships between keyworkers and service users and the processes involved, is the start of actively working within the network and life space of the service user. Chapter 9 examines this in relation to the process of matching in more detail. The sense of purpose and joy that can accompany the creation of a relationship and the sense of loss on changing keyworkers should not be minimised. The context of keyworking is one of engagement with supportive networks in living. The quality of the relationship will largely determine effectiveness.

The amount of social support that a relationship is able to bring and sustain will determine the degree to which stress in life may be coped with. Trust and empathy are important elements here. The feeling that one may share one's life in confidence will help. Giving confidence, increasing self esteem and a belief in the ability to cope are aspects of this.

EFFECTIVE RELATIONSHIPS IN SOCIAL CARE

Research indicates that a number of factors will be involved in determining how relationships like these are determined. The question is how individuals may be enabled to create effective relationships and how structures may be created to ensure that standards may be met:

- Following Goffman (1961) the role and the required performance of the keyworker should be clear within the norms of the setting. Goffman states that a *role* is 'the typical response of individuals in a particular position'. The orientation of setting devolves into *activities* and determines the *style of worker-user interaction* and the *outcomes of care*.
- Sutton (1979) found that *role performance* was partially determined by an implicit process in which individuals weigh up costs and benefits. These included:
    - perceptions and expectations of what is involved;
    - anticipated outcomes and expectations of benefit and cost;
    - considerations based upon past experiences;
    - personal values;
    - personal factors such as demands upon time and energy;
    - availability of support networks etc.; and
    - other competing activities.
- Brown (1986) found that ratings of staff behaviour such as fairness, friendliness, helpfulness, sense of humour, trust and confidence were *predictive indicators of positive outcomes*. The amalgam of all individual relationships was found to be predictive of *team performance*.
- Clough (1986) states that 'account must be taken not only of the fact that a service is performed but also of the manner in which the service is performed'.
- Truax and Carkhuff (1967) found that effective *personal relationships* of quality that have the capacity to produce change do so via, *accurate empathy, non-possessive warmth, authenticity* and *genuineness*.
- Kelly (1987) states that *relationships* 'are the fabric of all establishments, weaving together personalities and the interrelationships of users and other users, users and

staff, staff and staff'. The issues of *power, participative decision-making, the value base* of the setting and the *limitations of role* and *involvement* are dimension highlighted.

- *Individual accountability* within *relationships* rather than just *responsibility* is one of the strengths of keyworking. *Structures* and *systems* may be utilised to make services more accountable. Beresford and Croft (1986) argue for a dialogue; 'two way continuing processes rather than one – sided one – off snapshots'. In *relationships* , it appears a high degree of *equality*, *trust* and *shared agendas* are required.
- Rivlin (1983) argues that 'we are accountable to the people we work *with* and not *for*... (Thus) real power in residential units... (should) lie with residents'. *Responsibility* for *leadership* is placed here on managers of establishments and *responsibility* in relation to individual service users on keyworkers. Agreement as to the *purpose* of *relationships* and the *equality* or otherwise contained in them will form the basis of any ability for *participation in decision-making.*
- The *abuse of power* in some establishments may be indicated by *rules* (written or unwritten) that exercise *control*. Although *rules* and *sanctions* may be required, they should be made and *monitored* by the service user group.
- Douglas and Payne (1987) explore the relationship between *policies*, and *working arrangements* in relation to the *creation of rules and staff power*. Fennell (1986) shows how *power creation* (based upon compensatory notions, inaccessibility, hidden agendas, dependency and control) within *relationships* may be very real and in many circumstances destructive.
- Following Menzies (1967) factors such as *rules*, *ritualisation* and *detachment* may not be intentional, rather may consist of *social defences* by workers against anxiety.
- Clark and Asquith (1985) comment how in theory power

'...will tend to acquire legitimacy with the passing of time, and thus take on the aspect of authority'. Bettelheim (1974) found that *professionalism* is often used as a defence and thus is not professional.
- *Power* and *responsibilities* in keyworker systems are linked to *rights*. Following Gardner (1987), *participation* in care *decisions* and an *accountable* open system in which *decisions* take place need to be built into keyworking structures.

Research by the author (Mallinson, 1993) undertaken in residential care for older people, covered aspects of mutual trust, respect and participative decision-making. These are required in relationships between keyworkers and service users. The research drew out the following points:

- Time with service users needs to be spent by keyworkers in small living groups.
- Effective relationships will focus upon the quality of the service user's experience. Expectations and priorities need spelling out here by management.
- Service users need involvement in decisions through relationships with the keyworker. Decisions may focus on the notion of the provision of a service by keyworkers.
- The promotion and cultivation of special (jointly shared) interests may give a particular focus to the relationship.
- Supervision focusing clearly and consistently upon the quality of the service user's experience will create a sense of purpose.
- Keyworkers have a role in resolving tensions between individuals and groups. The general focus may be seen as the quality of user's experience in enhancing relationships and group interaction.
- Participation in decision-making should be seen in relation to accountability in the keyworker/ service user relationship, and in everyday practice in the provision of a service of quality by keyworkers.
- In sharing decisions between the service user, keyworker and supervisor the rights of users, evaluation of the

quality of the service and accountability may create a sense of focus.

- Positive relationships will build on the context of small group living. The quality of the service user's experience is important in enabling this. Relationships and group interaction may be said to be linked. The keyworker role as advocate of service user need and shared decision-making may help to create purposeful relationships.
- Promotion and cultivation of areas of common interest between service users and keyworkers may help to strengthen relationships.

These findings may be utilised to develop various aspects of the structures of keyworker systems.

ACHIEVING SOUND INDIVIDUALISED CARE AND RELATIONSHIPS

A checklist for development

Critical questions need to be asked by keyworkers and their managers if they are to achieve systems that will adequately meet individual needs:

- Are *priorities in the role* of keyworkers firmly established?
    - By clear *decision-making* techniques?
    - In appropriate *fora*?
    - By *discussing issues* with:
      Service users?
      Colleagues?
      Supervisor?
      Service user's family?
- Are individual keyworkers clear about their *role* and *expectations* in relation to:
    - *Assessment*: pre-admission *visits* and recommendations?
    - *Recording*?
    - *Care planning*?
      e.g. as manager of a care plan? or in *coordination* and *review*?

  - Deciding individual *special needs*?
  - Possible initial hearer of *complaints*?
  - Attending to *basic necessities*?
  - Delegated attention to *problem areas*?
  - *Filtering* through what is important or not?
  - Organising *outings*?
  - Involvement of service users in *social activities*?
  - Welcoming *relatives*?
  - *Talking through issues* with relatives?
  - Getting to know the finer points of service users' *likes and dislikes*?
  - Involving the *family*?
- Where keyworkers undertake *extra responsibility* is this clearly defined?
- Are arrangements made for *cover in the absence of keyworkers?*
- Where applicable, is there a development of the relationship of keyworking to *small living groups*?
- Are *expectations made clear* by:
  - A creative view of the *task*?
  - Creating a focus for *particular needs*?
  - *Matching* keyworker skills to *particular needs*?
  - *Enabling staff* to work with a small number of service users?
  - Enabling *communal decision-making*?
  - Actively helping *communication*?
  - Localising *relationships*?
  - Carrying out *group tasks* in relation to *individualised* care?
  - As a focus for *decision-making*?
  - In resolving tensions in group living via *consultative intervention*?
  - Enabling *relationships* outside the keyworker system?
- Are *contacts* (e.g. with the family) fully maintained by keyworkers?

- Do the arrangements for *matching* keyworkers and service users fully allow for:
    - Development of *relationships*?
    - Service user *choice*?
    - *Shared interests*?
    - Service users' *abilities* and particular *needs*?
    - Shared *decision-making*?
- Does the system allow for *issues to be discussed* and *tackled* in the *keyworker / service user relationship,* for example:
    - Differential *communication* with different service users?
    - Enabling *comfort and security*?
    - Knowing the service user well and what is happening to them?
    - *Responsibility* of keyworker?
    - Expectations based upon *mutual trust*?
    - Service user *choice*?
    - Working as a *community*?
    - *Accountability*?
    - Establishing *priorities*?
    - Establishing *rapport* with relatives?
    - Being *proactive*?
    - Establishing *relationships* of quality?
    - Maintaining *individuality*?
    - Being able to *sit down and talk*?
    - Providing *continuity of care*?
- Does the system allow for *issues to be discussed* and *tackled* between *keyworker* and *relatives, for example*:
    - *Availability* to talk to?
    - *Involvement* in planning?
    - Providing a point of *contact*?
    - In absence of keyworker asking other staff if anything is wanted?
    - *Accountability*?
    - Getting to really know the *service user*?
    - Working as one of the *family*?

- Has the *role performance* of individual keyworkers been maximised?
- Are *individual preferences* of service users met?
- Do *personal relationships* reflect:
  - *Empathy*?
  - *Authenticity*?
  - *Genuineness*?
  - *Equality*?
  - *Trust*?
  - *Shared agendas*?
- Are *anti-racist practice, attitudes* and *behaviour* promoted?
- Do *relationships* promote:
  - *Participation*?
  - *Power-sharing*?
  - *Service-user rights*?
  - *Independence*?
  - *Communication*?
  - *Support*?
  - Clarity in meeting *service user wishes*?
  - *Advocacy* and *service user power*?
  - *Partnership* and *choice*?
  - *Service user involvement*?
  - *Accountability*?
- Is *consumer* feedback/participation enabled in relationships? For example, by:
  - *Participative* decision-making?
  - *Involving* the service user:
  - In long term *planning*?
  - In day to day *events*?
  - Are indicators of *positive achievement* clear?
- Is the tension between *conflicting group* and *individual needs* resolved by debate and involvement of the service user group?
- Is individual care promoted within a sense of *corporate accountability* for the *outcomes* of *care*? Is this achieved by:
  - *Power-sharing*?

    - Clear policies shaping *action* and *relationships*?
    - *Participative decision-making*?
    - Agreed statements on common *values* for the setting?
    - The *design* of the system?
- Are individual inputs seen in relationship to overall *team performance*? Is this achieved by:
    - *Corporate accountability*?
    - Examining *roles* in relation to *power structures*?
    - Elaborating service user *rights*?
    - Service user *involvement*?
    - *Participation*?
    - *Empowerment*?
    - *Choice*?
    - *Responsiveness* to needs?

Five

Care planning in keyworker systems

INTRODUCTION

A cornerstone of an effective keyworker system is planning. In a structured approach emphasising the contractual nature of the service provided, the individual care plan defines personal needs identified by service users in conjunction with keyworkers and ways of meeting them are specified and coordinated. A care plan is thus an action plan. Individual care planning is a practical activity that:

- gives a sense of purpose to meeting needs;
- takes action in advance of any problems;
- ensures that service users do not get overlooked.

The keyworker is the person responsible for planning and coordinating the individualised package of personalised care of the service user. The range of responsibilities involved in care planning may, in some settings, be divided between the keyworker and their supervisor working jointly on an agreed basis.

AGREEMENTS IN SOCIAL CARE SETTINGS

The service user's individual care plan, as continually reviewed and updated is developed in the context of agreements made about the overall purpose of the setting.

Social care planning should thus be carried out on two levels: on an individual basis and across the service as a whole. Personal needs can be defined by service users in conjunction with keyworkers and ways of meeting them identified and coordinated. At the same time, overall philosophies of care should be set out in agreed statements; decision-making processes should involve all personnel directly involved.

The prospectus or publicity brochure for the service sets the tone and context of individual care planning. The agreement with the user on the initial receipt of the service may take the form of an itemised statement of specific individualised provision linked to the overall prospectus. Thus, the rights and responsibilities of both service users and staff may be laid out in the prospectus in everyday language, with suitable provision for minority languages and for visually impaired people.

For example in residential care the prospectus may state that: 'No member of staff will enter your room without permission'. 'Your privacy will be respected at all times'. 'Residents have a regular say in the everyday running of the home at meetings with staff'. Facilities available can be listed e.g. prayer, religious services, chiropody, hairdressing, and personal laundry resources. Each group of service users and their keyworker(s) will develop their own unique living arrangements according to the wishes expressed by users. Decisions here might include menus, routines, and new furnishings.

At the same time there may be a formal agreement between the setting and the purchaser of the service (e.g. care manager and/or service contractor). In social care settings (whether or not a care manager is involved) it is particularly helpful to plan to meet service user needs by monitoring progress against overall objectives agreed with the service user. Settings do however often monitor arrangements on behalf of care managers. Localised objectives may thus be agreed in plans devised within residential, day care and domiciliary care settings under the overall plan set by the care manager. The detailed daily knowledge of service users that is necessary for planning by care managers is really only gained through daily contact. Keyworkers feed information directly into individual programme planning or into reviews but sometimes may do this indirectly via care managers.

PRINCIPLES OF SOCIAL CARE PLANNING

Care planning should be conducted with a clarity of purpose. It should be a team function that pools expertise and concerns. It involves the commitment of all participants, and the sharing of expectations. Any possible differences of view will need acknowledging. Key objectives are:

- to enable the exercise of personal choice by service users in all decision-making and in all aspects of daily living including meeting individual needs;
- to recognise the uniqueness of each and every service user as an individual and the individual nature of their needs;
- to enable service users to take the highest degree of responsibility for their affairs that is possible;
- to promote openness between keyworkers and service users throughout all the process of social caring;
- to inform all service users of their rights and promote open discussion of the responsibilities that rights bring;
- to enable service users to develop skills in problem-solving, decision-making and assertiveness;
- to strive to maximise the service user's independence;
- to actively encourage service users to make their own choices, from a range of options, based upon informed risk taking;

- to acknowledge the general needs (for example health, personal hygiene, clothing, hair care) of service users reflecting these needs in provision as a whole.

The process of planning involves:

- shared decision-making and agreement between the service user, family and staff;
- clearly stated benefits to the service user;
- the keyworker and the agency working in close cooperation with the network of all those involved in the service user's welfare (e.g. individuals and institutions in the locality or community);
- purposeful intervention on the service user's behalf;
- clear statements of achievable long term goals and short term objectives;
- clear statements of the methods required to achieve these objectives;
- clear statements of how it will be known when goals have been achieved and what are acceptable outcomes;
- details of any constraints which may be imposed and that affect the achievement of goals, and how these are to be addressed;
- an agreed timescale for review.

Part of the skill of the keyworker is the clear assessment of need. This will be required to take into account the service user's norms of culture and class. It includes the identification of the changes in the service user's situation that they most desire and that all involved are most strongly motivated to achieve. Meeting cultural needs e.g. meals, and prayers and the development of self image are very real to users and yet easily overlooked.

Ordinary events like sharing a meal or helping a person into bed become a medium for defining needs and for establishing a framework for intervention. The keyworker's task is to become acutely aware of how, as a unique individual a particular person functions; what they feel about their situation; what they feel their needs are; how their needs may be met and how decisions may be translated into action.

The initial stages of care planning involve collecting information; assessment; definition of issues with the service user; identification of the methods and resources required to achieve change, and establishing the agreed baseline against which possible outcomes can be measured.

An exploration of the willingness of all relevant people to join in the change process is required. The agency's commitment to bring about change should also be clarified. In establishing the 'contractual' commitment of all parties, account should be taken of fears and anxieties. Differences of views and opinion can be recorded as an open recognition that they exist.

On implementation, any necessary support and encouragement detailed in the plan, will be required. The primary roles of the keyworker here are coordinator and advocate, as well as participant.

If the goals stated in care plans are to be realistic, the change that they express should be readily demonstrated. In successful evaluation any change that has occurred is readily apparent. For example, the effect of a 'reduction in distress' may be indicated by 'improved sleep at night' and by 'less time spent isolated and weeping'. These indicators are quantifiable and clear. Thus, 'before and after' pictures can be obtained upon which keyworkers and service users can monitor and evaluate the effectiveness of the implementation of a care plan.

Objectives should be focused and very specific. They need to be 'sharp' and express immediacy so that they become a motivating factor. They should be satisfying as a contribution to a sense of self esteem. They are concerned with provable outcomes and not with process.

In monitoring effectiveness on a continuing basis, diaries and record sheets may be used. Supervision can be used to reflect upon these and upon the personal development of the service user.

Basic questions on review are: Do the issues still exist? Has there been any deterioration or improvement in condition? What has been the outcome of intervention? How effective was the process? Is further work required on these issues? The termination or the drafting of a further care plan should then follow, as is appropriate to the circumstances of the individual.

Framework for a Care Plan

1. Summary of the service user's current situation and needs.
2. Long term goals.
3. Short term objectives.
4. Methods of achieving objectives.
5. The nature of specific issues upon which it is proposed to work.
6. Baseline in relation to objectives.
7. Outcomes expected.
8. Constraints upon intervention and how these are to be addressed.
9. Resources required.
10. Action required by the various parties involved.
11. Role of the keyworker.
12. Role of the supervisor.
13. Mechanisms for the monitoring of the achievement of objectives.
14. Methods of evaluation.
15. Proposed timing and mode of review.

If all these practice principles (reflecting concepts such as choice, and individualisation) are followed the benefits of keyworking to service users will become apparent. Such benefits include:

- having a personal agent;
- a personalised service;
- continuity of care;
- regular review;
- improved recording; and
- personal care plans.

There are also benefits here for keyworkers:

- improved job satisfaction and interest;
- greater ability to cope with stress;
- better understanding of service user's needs;
- better communication networks;
- improved development opportunities;
- even distribution of work; and
- recognition of personal achievement.

The setting up of any keyworker system will involve talking through these principles with the staff involved. Particular attention will need to be given to issues such as choice, consumer participation and the rights of keyworkers and service users. The nature of good practice in the areas of confidentiality and effective and ethical recording needs to be considered. Meeting cultural needs of service users should form a key part of systems. Issues here are race, gender, age and religion. Keyworking if it is to be effective must take on board all these issues in the context of the relationships within the staff and user team.

EFFECTIVE CARE PLANNING

It is useful to review general research findings so that effectiveness of individual keyworkers may be increased, and structures devised for care planning within keyworker systems placed upon secure ground.

In general terms research shows that effective care planning will involve:

- values that respect choice, dignity, rights, fulfilment, privacy and independence;
- joint monitoring and evaluation;
- decision-making involving service users;
- the recognition of differing perspectives;
- involvement and challenge;
- working with the strengths of the service user's situation;
- interdependence of person, behaviour and environment.

Some specific findings are now summarised.
Following Allen-Meares and Lane (1987):

- Decision-making is based upon *personalised relationships*, in the context of the setting as a whole.
- *Assessment decisions* are influenced by 'complex interrelationships that exist between people and their environments'. *Relationships*, *groups/group living*, and transitions, form part of this.
- Behaviour may be dependent upon the nature of a setting.
- A keyworker *systems* may be used to create, structured relationships.
- *Assessment data* may include a wide range of factors in the care setting, community, and other aspects of living. It gives an integrated and comprehensive picture of the service user's situation linked to *intervention strategies* at a variety of critical points and levels within the systems involved.
- The keyworker is the *mediator* between the service user and their environment in the context of a *personalised relationship*.

According to Hanvey (1987):

- *Language* and *communication* may be used as a motivating force.
- Problems need translating into action.
- Strengths may be built upon within *relationships* rather than weaknesses highlighted.
- A system should include informal *monitoring* and *evaluation* of *assessment* and intervention to establish progress, as well as formal *reviews*.

Farrar and Tierney (1985) state that 'It may be difficult for a social worker to stand back and view...intervention with objectivity... [The] ...worker can become 'enmeshed' in the client's problems'. They thus advocate *joint evaluation* by worker, supervisor and service user.

Hulley (1985) states that:

- Keyworking blends the *roles* of *enabler* and *advocate*. Deciding priorities here is the service user's prerogative.
- Review meetings 'should be called for a purpose...apparent to all'.
- *Responsibility* and *accountability* may be achieved within *trusted relationships* rather than the *bureaucratic* machine.
- Purposeful *reviews* have *clear outcomes* and are based upon *personalised user-based decision-making*.

Kelly and Beck (1990) maintain that meeting need should generally reflect *user choice* and variations between users. *Service objectives* and principles should be clearly stated. In purposeful *intervention* the success of everyday practice may be seen in the achievement of the *objectives* of *individual care plans*.

This is echoed in Jones (1968) where for residential care, the principle of *decision-making* by *consensus* is formulated. Keyworker systems need to make:

- explicit statements about *values* and *relationships* in relation to *decision-making*;
- Evaluations that concern *participation* and *involvement*;
- the *outcomes* of all *individual care plans* clear in relation to the *processes* and *structures* of the setting as a whole.

According to Coulshed (1990), individual and organisational decision-making in the planning process should:

- recognise implicit values and assumptions;
- if possible, involve everyone concerned;
- be understandable and communicated clearly;
- be translated into specific objectives at all relevant levels;
- state who is responsible for implementing the action plan;
- indicate target dates for achievement;
- spell out the intended effects and predicted costs;
- deal with implications for training and for other agencies;

- offer some degree of flexibility/ discretion;
- decide if a contingency plan is needed;
- decide who will monitor, evaluate and review the plans.

According to Darvill and Smale (1990) care plans should take into account the need for a wide network of contact and support in the service user's life. The partnership between service user and keyworkers should reflect this, as should the activities and goals of the care plan. Taking into account the whole network of those involved or who could be involved should be based upon a problem solving approach.

The author's own research (Mallinson, 1993) makes the following points in relation to the keyworker as the coordinator of the care plan and in relation to decision-making:

- The keyworker should focus upon the quality of user's experience. Clear and consistent supervision is the key to enabling this.
- Care planning may promote accountability.
- Keyworkers may enable networks and promote effective involvement of relatives.
- Keyworkers may act as advocates of service user need.
- Shared decision-making may be promoted in the keyworker service user relationship, and between user, keyworker and supervisor.
- Needs may be interpreted through keyworker discussions with relatives.
- Supervision may be used to focus upon the quality of user's experience.
- The rights of users provide a focus for effective decision-making.

STAGES IN CARE PLANNING

A number of stages are involved in care planning by keyworkers. These are now outlined.

1. **Getting to know you**: the keyworker will spend some time with the service user explaining what a care plan is

and that they need to know them better in order to fully meet their needs. If the service user agrees to be involved in planning, the keyworker builds a picture of major influences, events, likes and dislikes.

2. **The action plan**: the keyworker assesses with their supervisor and the service user what is needed to improve the quality of life of the service user. A plan of action is then formulated. The plan is shared with the team and strategies considered to bring it about.
3. **Putting the plan into practice**: in the process of everyday living the plan provides a framework that gives the task of the worker a sense of clarity and focus. It can be used to motivate the service user to change aspects of their lifestyle that were agreed should be modified. It gives a sense of direction to all concerned. Progress should be monitored and noted.
4. **Reviewing progress**: the care plan is reviewed regularly. This may take place in team meetings, say once or twice per year, or in supervision as often as it may be necessary.

1. Getting to know you

If keyworkers know users well they will find it easy to formulate a care plan.

In discussions with users about their background and experiences, keyworkers may find it helpful to focus upon understanding significant events. Photographs are examples of a medium to encourage discussion. This will help to create a positive relationship.

Areas that may be discussed include:

- family and cultural background;
- early life;
- employment;
- relationships;
- significant life events and experiences.

Keyworkers will need to assess the residents current situation and needs. They may wish to focus upon the following needs:

Social
Physical
Intellectual
Cultural
Emotional and
Spiritual

Supervisors may help by giving the 'space' for workers to create relationships. They can use supervision to reflect upon user's needs, the meaning that a care plan may have for a user and what can be done to 'make things happen'.

Strengths in the users circumstances need acknowledging, weaknesses may be worked upon so that the quality of life can be improved.

2. From values to action

Having considered the nature of the user's situation and their social history, the keyworker may assess what should to be done by the establishment in order to improve the quality of life of the resident.

It is useful to first assess how key values are practised, and the extent to which they meet the interests or needs of the resident. Key values include:

- **Rights:** the rights of residents to basic freedoms should be safeguarded.
- **Privacy:** residents should have the right to privacy whenever they want it.
- **Dignity:** resident's self respect should be safe-guarded and their personal needs respected.
- **Choice:** residents should be free to make their own decisions.
- **Independence:** residents should be able to retain as much independence as possible including the right to take personal risks.
- **Fulfilment:** residents should be enabled to achieve their potential capacity – physical, intellectual, emotional and social.

The aims of the plan should be written down and how they are to be achieved.

Issues as to whether the plan is to be formalised, where it is to be kept, how it will be reviewed and whose responsibility it is to carry things through will all need to be agreed.

3. Putting the plan into practice

It is one thing having a plan, it is another carrying it out.

The keyworker or their supervisor will need to be clear who is working with particular objectives. There will need to be agreed ways that the plan will be coordinated and put into action. This will need to be regularly monitored.

Monitoring involves supporting the achievement of set objectives over time and adapting the care plan to the changing needs of the user. A number of different tasks are involved:

- monitoring care plan objectives;
- coordinating inputs;
- overseeing the quality of care;
- supporting the service users and carers;
- contributing to the review process.

4. Reviewing progress

This stage makes sure that objectives have been met or that they are reviewed if they are no longer appropriate. It may establish a new plan to suit changed needs.

A number of differing purposes of a review meeting may therefore be expressed:

- reviews the achievement of care plan objectives;
- examines the reasons for success or failure;
- evaluates the quality of care provided;
- reassesses current needs;
- revises care plan objectives;
- redefines service requirements;
- sets the date for the next review; and
- records the findings of the review.

ACHIEVING SOUND CARE PLANNING

A checklist for development of structures

Keyworking provides the medium in which creative and effective care planning can take place. The setting up of the networks required for implementation of the care plan are part of the keyworker's role as manager and coordinator of the care plan. Service user's personal choice in daily living and high levels of service user decision-making should be actively facilitated. Questions will need to be asked by keyworkers, supervisors and managers if they are to achieve keyworker systems that adequately reflect requirements to plan for individual needs and to adequately frame decision-making:

- Is there a clear *policy* on *involvement* of keyworkers in *planning and review*?
  - Has the basis of the *main tasks* of keyworkers been fully elaborated and discussed?
  - Has work been *prioritised*?
  - Have ways of working been *determined* with the service user?
  - Are *relatives involved*?
  - Is *joint work* between keyworker and supervisor promoted?
  - How are *service user's wishes* to be interpreted?
  - How is *assessment* to be conducted?
  - Does keyworking *get beyond* concentration on *physical care*?
  - How does the system work in any *absence* of the keyworker?
  - Are there clear *targets* and *objectives* for keyworkers?
- In *planning for the setting* as a whole are policies and action promoted within the keyworker system in relation to:
  - *Groups/group living*?
  - *Transitions*?
  - *Purpose of care*?
  - *Philosophy* of setting?

  - *Participation* and *involvement*?
  - *Personalised relationships*?
  - *Joint evaluation* by worker, supervisor and service user?
  - *Language* and *communication*?
  - *Enabling* and *advocacy*?
  - *Responsibility* and *accountability*?
  - *Service-user decision-making*?
  - *Service-user rights*?
  - *Participation* and *involvement*?
  - *Differing perspectives*?
- Does the *assessment* and *intervention process* include:
  - Identification of personal needs by the service user?
  - *Joint monitoring and evaluation*?
  - *Service user decision-making*?
  - Service user *choice*?
  - Ability to accommodate *differing perspectives*?
  - Clear *planning*?
  - Service user's *rights*?
  - Service user *involvement* and *challenge*?
  - *Participatory decision-making*?
  - Working with the *strengths* of the service user's situation?
  - *Interdependence* of *person*, *behaviour* and *environment*?
  - Working with the *family system*?
  - *Clear benefits* to the service user?
  - Definition of *realistic* and *achievable goals*?
  - Working through constraints?
  - Involving and working with networks of relationships?
  - Achieving *independence and fulfilment*?
- Does the process of *review of intervention* include:
  - *A clear focus upon outcomes*?
  - Joint evaluation and monitoring?
  - An *agreed timescale*?
  - *Choice in service user decision-making*?

- Service user *involvement*?
- Clear *accountability of staff*?
- A focus upon the *personal experience* of the service user?
- Discussion of the reasons for *success or failure*?
- A *reappraisal of needs*?

Six

Teamwork in keyworker systems

INTRODUCTION

Decision-making in keyworker systems is carried out through the staff team. Teamwork is concerned with the integration of work practices and relationships. Whilst keyworking concerns individualisation and personalisation of care this is always carried out in a group context (in terms of service users and/ or staff). Thus teamwork is a crucial thread going through all keyworking practice. The task may be clearly laid down but the role of the keyworker will also depend upon expectations of other team members.

Teamwork will give support to staff and create clear shared consensual ways of working. Teamwork does not just happen, it has to be worked for and worked towards. The interrelationship within teams will provide a wider basis for keyworking. The shared decision-making within the staff team creates a brief beyond individualisation. The group nature of provision or settings requires teamwork if effective working is to be the result.

Effective teamwork will minimise the possible problems which can exist in some keyworker systems. Such problems may include:

- competitiveness between workers;
- issues of keyworker absence and arranging cover;
- any power differential between service users and keyworkers, and in turn, management;
- the danger of keyworkers imposing their own values and interests upon 'their' service users;
- superficial involvement of other staff;
- the induction of new keyworkers and difficulties inherent in the familiarisation of new keyworkers with the existing service user group.

A shared platform for support and development, for group decision-making, and for effective provision, is thus the essence of teamwork.

THE PRINCIPLES OF TEAMWORK

A range of principles for teamwork will include:

- a clearly identified purpose;
- common aims and goals established through clear objectives that are regularly reviewed;
- co-operation and collaboration between members;
- interdependence of team members based upon common aims and trust built through working relationships and a shared task;
- complementary roles and functions of team members;
- an identified strategy for achieving aims and objectives;
- criteria for measuring effectiveness;
- evaluation and monitoring of performance and strategy;
- clear lines of communication and procedures;
- problem solving as a group function in a co-operative, supportive environment;
- a high degree of identity, cohesion and stability;
- a sense of openness, support and trust;
- a cohesive work group with relationships that seek to

openly work through conflict giving mutual support;
- accountable practice established through involving consumer representation.

EFFECTIVE TEAMWORK

These principles were based upon a survey of major research and theoretical works. Some of these are explored below. Factors in effective teamwork appear to be:

- *Staff cohesion* which is said to be a potent factor in the *effectiveness* of teams in group care (Johnson, 1981, 1982).
- The quality of *teamwork* is said to contribute to the *efficiency and effectiveness* of the whole (Morrison, 1986). 'Individuals should be asked to specify openly what help and support they want from the team... (so that they can) ...begin to develop effective communication patterns which are essential to coordinated and co-operative working'.
- Pope (1982) focuses the argument upon clarity and simplicity in *aims*, clear lines of *communication*, an adequate pattern of *support*. Similarly, Dunham (1980) on *communication* and *cooperation* between professionals involved.
- Essential dimensions of teamwork that become the building blocks of development, are according to Woodcock's approach (1979):
    - *clear objectives and goals*;
    - *openness* and *confrontation*;
    - *support* and *trust*;
    - *cooperation and conflict*;
    - *sound procedures*;
    - *appropriate leadership*;
    - *regular review*;
    - *individual development*; and
    - *sound inter-group relations.*
- In creating *participative working practices*, Douglas et al. (1988) highlight the need for greater *consistency* between

formal and informal work practices, involving consumers, the need for *boundaries*, working through *contradictions and conflicts*; and the need for *common agreements* on issues.

- Johnson (1981) in researching key variables in the residential milieu found that varying *levels of staff cohesion* significantly affected the *quality and standard* of the *work* of settings. In particular:
  - *support*;
  - *personal problem-orientation*, (the extent to which service users are encouraged to examine personal problems and feelings);
  - *autonomy* (the decision-making power of the users);
  - *practical orientation* (i.e. orientation towards practical goals and general skill – building); and
  - *staff control* (the extent to which staff use rules, schedules and other measures to control users).
- Johnson (1982) surveys the USA literature on *staff cohesion* and suggests that *positive open professional relationships* resolving *value conflicts* and giving *mutual support* are prerequisites for sound residential practice. In the UK, Burt (1985) reinforces this view as *staff relationships* will affect *personal relationships* with service users. Burt argues for *democratic leadership*, *team support* and *supervision*.
- Elliott (1982) highlights the importance of *consultation* within the team to offer *support*. In keyworker systems the *relationship* of the individual keyworker *to the team*, and the *support* the team gives may thus be the pivot point for effective *individualised* care in a group setting.

These findings have a direct bearing on the structure of keyworker systems.

THE TEAM AND THE INDIVIDUAL KEYWORKER

A team approach, according to the research we have just outlined, shares common work practices. Keyworkers are not just individual workers, they are part of the system of which the work group is a part. The team is responsible and accountable for the conduct of the system. Changes in the nature of the system are dependent for their effect upon each individual acting together within and as the group as a whole.

Members of the team will each bring into the work situation different sets of professional values, opinions, and skills. Time must be allowed for sharing, exploring and exchanging these viewpoints. Differing roles and goals need sharing so that an understanding and consensus is achieved as to why they are different, and how skills and expectations crucial to the success of the team may be developed.

Teamwork implies mutually independent contributions by keyworkers to the whole. It is important that the nature of that whole is debated and understood by all concerned. Each individual keyworker's contribution may then be placed in the overall context of the whole. In considering a team's effectiveness, the organisation should however acknowledge the balance between what is appropriate for the team and what is beneficial for individual performance of the keyworker and for their personal self esteem.

COMMUNICATION

Germane to the effectiveness of both keyworker systems, and keyworkers in teams, is the communication network. The quality of communication will determine the quality of keyworking. Poor communication, it goes without saying, will breed misunderstandings and poor practice. The issue however is broader than that, as it is the quality and style of the communication system as well as the individual practices within the system that is important.

In implementing a keyworker system, all the written records and the procedures for their use, should be overhauled to meet the needs of changing working practices. Small factors will take on a new significance as the roles and tasks of individuals change. Examples of this in residential care are passing crucial information between staff upon changes of shift, and channelling essential assessment information to keyworkers from colleagues. Clear guidelines devised and agreed by the workers themselves (so that they are committed to their maintenance and use) is the prescription here. The task of the team is to monitor their effectiveness across the whole establishment. Managers may thus include communication techniques in their staff development programmes.

According to Mitchell (1983) communication partially derives from motivation in that it reduces uncertainty, helps solve problems, confirms the nature of action and its effect, enables control of a situation, and gives feedback.

Thus as Atherton (1989) says 'the meaning of a communication is to be determined by its effect...communication is effected by behaviour'. It will form a central part of creating meaning in relationships (keyworker and user relationships, and those between keyworkers and supervisors). It is also a vital link between component parts of the keyworker system. The structure of routines will convey powerful messages reflecting the value base of the setting and of the management of the setting. The effect of communication is indicative of the culture of the setting. It is the team leader's task to create an appropriate and constructive culture, and a meaningful ethos in which positive communication flourishes.

TEAM LEADERSHIP

The main role of leadership in a team of keyworkers is to point the way to the team, identifying and symbolising what is important. The qualities, characteristics and skills demanded of the leader and the style of leadership are largely determined by the particular situation in which keyworking is practised. Sharing ideals and creating organisational pride will create a platform to enable people to realise their potential and to feel valued. Managing expectations and creating support are ways of ensuring that there are adequate mechanisms to carry out the task

Research on leadership suggests the following social qualities demanded of successful leaders:

- ability to enlist co-operation;
- administrative ability;
- attractiveness;
- cooperativeness;
- nurturance;
- popularity and prestige;
- sociability and interpersonal skills;
- social participation;
- tact and diplomacy.

Most of these are acquired qualities that the team leader should strive for. For example, effective leaders of teams of keyworkers are problem solvers rather than problem avoiders

Thus if one follows research by Coulshed (1990) a leader of keyworkers will be a person who:

- is considerate, friendly, supportive, fair, objective;
- is enthusiastic, builds confidence and inspiration in others;
- gives credit where it is due, and appreciates suggestions and ideas;
- encourages participation in decision-making;
- lets the team know what is expected of them;
- sets specific goals, measures progress and gives concrete feedback;
- is aware of training and development needs and gives concrete feedback;
- keeps everyone informed about decisions and developments;
- acts decisively in sorting out work-related problems;
- delegates authority and responsibility appropriately;
- emphasises the importance of each person working at his or her best;
- devises plans in advance and makes contingency plans;

- makes sure that the team coordinates its activities;
- enables the team to get on with its work;
- helps to settle conflicts and disagreements amongst the team members;
- takes action if people do not pull their weight or violate the rules;

Following Adair (1973) any leader of keyworkers who focuses upon the task in hand will also need to:

- *plan*: defining the group task and individual keyworker's task(s) making them workable;
- *initiate*: briefing, explaining aims, allocating tasks and setting standards, focusing clearly upon processes to achieve clear outcomes in service user care;
- *control*: maintaining standards, ensuring action is taken;
- *support*: encouraging, creating team spirit, exploring disagreements making sure keyworkers work together as a team;
- *inform*: clarifying plans and action, giving and receiving information, summarising suggestions;
- *evaluate*: checking feasibility of ideas, testing out consequences of action, examining performance, helping individual keyworkers and the group evaluate.

TEAM AND INDIVIDUAL DEVELOPMENT

As we have seen, individual and collective needs, in relation to the requirements of the setting, focus upon a team approach. A number of functions may be stated in the development of that approach by leaders within keyworker systems (see Douglas and Payne, 1988, who develop work by Bertcher and Garvin, 1969):

- In *induction*, to develop appropriate and effective ways of introducing keyworkers and teams to their work.
- In *re-orientation*, to assist staff in taking on new roles and responsibilities as additional duties are delegated or systems change.

- In *providing continuing learning opportunities*, undertaking regular and systematic reassessment of needs.
- In *meeting organisational demands*, developing knowledge and skills in agency procedures and processes demand regular updating.
- In *updating* staff the leader should ensure that they are kept up to date with changing service needs, new knowledge, professional approaches etc.
- In *building and developing the team*, concentration upon skills in working together with other agencies and disciplines is required.
- In pursuing *regular evaluation*, the leader should ensure that staff are continually relating to their work care goals and tasks and learning to modify them and to change their practice as a result.

Team building programmes may be required in order to facilitate these. The rationale here, according to Collins and Bruce (1984) is clear: if a team works together more effectively then they will achieve primary organisational goals more efficiently. They suggest that the first stage in team building is achieving commitment and consensus upon what is needed to be done and organising appropriate programmes based upon clear frameworks and goals. This may be followed by individual discussions of what the development agenda means for individual keyworkers. Analysis of the team's strengths and weaknesses creates an agenda to be worked upon.

There is not sufficient space to detail the many possibilities here. The reader is directed for this to works such as Woodcock (1979) and Douglas and Payne (1987). Giving feedback and evaluation is part of this process. Following Collins and Bruce (1984) common issues that often have to be tackled are:

- conflict over the nature of the task and roles within it;
- defining organisational policy and setting realistic goals;
- effective management of interpersonal and

interprofessional relationships (e.g. bringing out hidden agendas and negotiating conflict);
- improving communication; and
- providing appropriate levels of interpersonal sensitivity and support.

Finding ways to manage work related stress and anxiety is often seen as a prominent factor in determining the level of institutional success (e.g. Menzies, 1967). Teams and supervisors will need to be mindful of factors in social care work that may exhaust keyworker's ability to cope. Examples here may be violent behaviour by emotionally damaged service users and settings that experience severe role conflict or move from one crisis to another. Managers and supervisors in the context of the team need to plan work, and facilitate internal support. Issues such as realistic job distribution, co-keyworking, team building and discussion of and sharing of problems are some ways forward.

According to Collins and Bruce (1984) team building in social care will need to cover the areas of:

- *Skills and learning*: this will be based upon interaction, acknowledging personal and professional strengths, sharing skills and tasks and respect amongst team members for differing ideas and values.
- *Support and responsibility*: this will be based upon establishing trust, co-operative working, tolerance, understanding and sensitivity, effective communication and personal feedback.
- *An effective emotional climate*: this will involve communication and awareness.
- *Clear organisation and policy*: thus will involve united aims, commitment to the task, and updating work methods.

ACHIEVING SOUND TEAMWORK IN KEYWORKER SYSTEMS

A checklist of areas for development

Crucial questions need to be asked by managers and members of the staff team if they are to work together effectively in order to meet the needs of service users:

Has *team functioning* in relation to keyworker systems been evaluated and promoted?

- Issues to be tackled are:
    - Clear lines of *communication*?
    - An adequate pattern of *support*?
    - Capacity to function as a *problem-solving group*?
    - High degree of *identity*?
    - *Cohesion*?
    - *Stability*? and *security*?
    - *Openness* and *confrontation*?
    - *Support* and *trust*?
    - *Cooperation*?
    - *Common agreement*?
- The promotion of:
    - *Sound procedures*?
    - *Inter-group relations*?
    - *Participative working*?
    - *Consistency* between *formal and informal*?
    - *Work practices*?
- Have the following *team practices* been considered in relation to keyworker systems:
    - *Communication*?
    - *Cooperation*?
    - *Individual development*?
    - Working through *contradictions and conflicts*?
    - *Pooling of information*?
    - *Establishing priorities*?
    - Considering *roles and* boundaries?
- Do the staff team work as a *cohesive* group? Aspects are:
    - *Relationships*?
    - Working through *conflict*?
    - Creating awareness of *problem solving*?
    - Keyworker *orientation to the team*?
    - *Positive open professional relationships*?
    - Resolving *value conflicts*?
    - Giving *mutual support*?

- Have common *aims and goals* been established by:
    - Clarity and simplicity in *aims*?
    - *Clear objectives and goals*?
    - *Regular review*?
    - Considering *individual development*?
    - *Consistency* between *formal and informal work*?
    - *Practices*?
    - *Involving consumers*?
    - *Establishing priorities*?
    - *Accountability*?

Seven

Managing keyworker systems

INTRODUCTION

The effectiveness of the practice of any team of keyworkers is largely determined by the quality of the way they are managed. Keyworkers will only work effectively if clear operational guidelines are given by managers within an enabling management style. Keyworkers need guidance and support if they are to do their job well.

Research shows that keyworking generally improves the standard of care, yet in a small number of cases the implementation of keyworker systems may actually lower standards. Poor management appears to be the cause of these problems. Without sound management even the most committed and capable worker will feel that they are wasting their time and their performance will drop accordingly.

This chapter aims to learn from these experiences and to highlight sound managerial practice.

EFFECTIVE MANAGEMENT IN KEYWORKER SYSTEMS

In working up a prescription for the effective management of keyworker systems, a review was made of research and other findings concerning social care. These findings are summarised below:

- Phillips (1986) makes clear the direct relationship between management tasks and the quality of the daily experiences of service users.
- *Leadership* in the oversight of teams will be required for keyworker systems to work effectively. Leger (1980) and Phillips (1986) indicate that the key areas of *policy*, *philosophy*, *supervision*, and *monitoring*, are central to such practice.
- Senior (1989) cites research by Burns and Stalker (1961) as evidence that *lateral communication* (between team members working and consulting together) rather than vertical communication based upon an autocratic hierarchy placing demands upon the workforce is the most effective way of managing. 'Creating a culture where... (keyworkers) are responsible to each other and to residents produces a far better practice than the usual policy of controlling through intermittent intervention from above'.
- A philosophy of anti-racist practice in the management of social care highlights many managerial tasks which contribute to an overall enabling style (see e.g. SCA, 1990) elements here are:
    - *Positive action*.
    - *Job enrichment* for all staff, recognising the diversity of skills and knowledge in individuals and the staff group.
    - Promoting *self-awareness*, enabling contributions based upon Black and white realities.
    - Promoting *positive change*, harnessing the abilities of staff.
    - Setting aims and objectives.
    - Defining the task and clarifying expectations.
    - Achieving common understanding.
- Leger (1980) states 'we should be looking for effective management which will provide a necessary

foundation...ensuring that the philosophy and purpose of the setting are clear by *identifying objectives, developing resources, defining staff roles and responsibilities* and *evaluating results*. There should be good *supervision* ... to give people added goals, encourage stability and development... '.

- Brown and Brearley (1990) suggest that *monitoring*, maintaining and developing *standards* is a primary part of the manager's task. A key issue was the methods and processes for coordinating monitoring.
- Leigh (1989) examines these issues in relation to the organisation's *culture* and *values*, confirming their importance and their clear relationship to sound management of keyworker systems.
- *Supervision* has been of central importance in the management of social work *teams*. Pettes (1979) allied *tasks* in *staff supervision* to *tasks* in *management*. Westheimer (1977) also saw the grounding it gave as a primary tool in the manager's repertoire to enable *standards* and the *effectiveness* or *quality of care* in settings. Other writers see supervision as a means of *support* (Braithwaite, 1988) and *development* of individuals and settings (Sills, 1988).
- Supervision may be linked to the management of work stressors. As the focus of issues such as *communication*, *control*, and *task orientation*, it is here that the tension between emotional demands and essential practical tasks is likely to be resolved. Research by Siddiqui (1991) shows that these are the most common determinants of *work-related stress* in residential homes for older people, hence the need for managers to know their staff as individuals.
- *Supervision* as a vehicle to facilitate *Planning* was highlighted in research by Vernon and Fruin (1986). The role was seen as an *enabling process* rather than just one of administration or monitoring. Despite problems derivative of poor practice in some settings, supervision has a key role in *maintaining and developing effectiveness*.

- Tavener (1989) found supervision to be a key process that both reflects and feeds into *management style*. In the tension between *bureaucracy* and *professionalism*, the supervisor appears to be able enable people to learn new ways and new ideas and to *change agency* practice.
- Carrol and Tosi (1973) found that people who are involved in *setting their own goals* are likely to show higher levels of *worker performance* than those whose goals are set for them. *Feedback*, if it is specific, tactful and immediate, tends to lead to an improvement in *performance* (Locke et al., 1981).
- Tosi and Carroll (1968) also found that using an *objective-led approach* in *supervision* and *monitoring* let individuals know what was expected of them; it aided *planning* by *clarifying goals and targets*. Improved *communication* resulted whilst *evaluation* was more effective as people focused specifically upon goals and upon positive achievement.
- Unwin (1987) reviewed the research on *setting objectives* and found that the principles of *clarity, consultation, agreement on priorities,* some *team independence*, frequent *team review*, *supportive feedback*, and agreement on *evaluation measures* to be of benefit. *Clarity of expectations* between manager and keyworker is thus of importance.
- Research in the USA (Meyer, 1986) indicates that *job satisfaction* in residential settings is found when influence is available to staff in the areas of *decision-making* and the *characteristics* of job design.

The author's own research (Mallinson, 1993) makes the following findings in relation to effective supervision and evaluation in keyworker systems:

- a firm managerial agenda will be linked to notions of the everyday task;
- supervision will actively draw out individual issues;
- a notion of accountability of all concerned should be developed;

- supervision will focus clearly and consistently upon the quality of user's experience;
- a framework for keyworker roles and tasks, setting standards and expectations may be enabled through supervision;
- management should promote shared decision-making in the keyworker service user relationship, enabling this to happen clearly in the everyday practice of keyworkers.

MANAGING SOCIAL CARE THROUGH KEYWORKER SYSTEMS

The wide range of tasks carried out by keyworkers thus need teamwork, supervision and support if they are to be carried out effectively. Well managed keyworking systems will enable sound communication, delegation, accountability and supervision.

Specific attention should therefore be given by managers to the following areas:

- clearly defining roles in conjunction with keyworkers to avoid role conflict and conflicting expectations;
- enabling good communication to be built into the system;
- factors such as rotas, shifts, cover and referral systems which should not be allowed to constrain the quality of the service;
- effective team and individual development;
- supervision, support and training;
- delegation of authority to keyworkers which should be clear and be given in an atmosphere of support;
- appraisal of performance and opportunities for personal development;
- accountability which should be clearly defined, including roles, responsibilities, and communication processes;
- close monitoring and review of the system's effectiveness and its efficient operation.

Keyworking should be based upon clearly defined roles; good communication systems, teamwork, planning, supervision, support and training; clear delegation of authority and clear philosophies of care.

Some specific areas of management are now examined in greater depth.

EFFICIENCY: A MANAGERIAL RATIONALE

Clearly defined roles promote a sense of structure and rationality. The review of keyworking by SCA/BASW (1987) found that when aims and objectives are precisely defined, keyworking can by used to promote efficiency. The inputs to the system can be clarified and the outputs more closely defined and results determined in both individual and collective terms. Such inputs include quantifiable amounts of staffing and other resources used to achieve definable outputs in relation to elements of the settings' overall purpose and philosophy of care.

Keyworking it may be maintained, also promotes the effectiveness of settings as they are able to meet clearly defined individual and collective needs and goals. For example, the evaluation by supervisors of keyworker's implementation of care plans can be used on a collective basis to ensure that the overall output of the unit achieves the desired results. Performance review of the achievement of care philosophies can be more readily achieved within keyworker systems. They are also more economical in relation to the task, in their use of scarce resources such as staffing hours.

The clear definition of requirements, goals and philosophies of care revolve around the introduction of keyworking as a system for care management. A clearer definition of inputs and outputs promotes a sense of clarity in the consideration of the attainment of efficiency and of effectiveness. Goal displacement and role conflict it is suggested, will be minimised if managers evaluate the operation of a system and monitor its effectiveness in a planned way.

The allocation of a keyworker to a service user does not however automatically guarantee that these other elements will follow. It is the linking of sound managerial evaluation and practice into keyworker systems that provides a framework for the promotion of efficiency (rather than keyworking pursued alone.) Keyworking provides a framework upon which to hang the requirements of sound managerial practice and planned service development.

Keyworker systems it has been found will be more efficient if they are themselves *specifically* designed with the ideas, focus and principles of economy, efficiency and effectiveness in mind.

The setting up of any system should thus address issues such as the acquisition of resources in appropriate quantity and quality at the lowest cost (economy); the maximisation of output for those resources (efficiency); and the ensuring that output achieves the desired result (effectiveness).

Such a system will need to obtain its focus from a number of principles. It will need to contain:

- a clear sense of direction;
- statements of aims and a commitment to achieving these;
- a planning process involving analysis, explicit standards, definition of the results required, periodic review, and contingency plans;
- policy review that systematically assesses the continuing relevance of the setting;
- planning mechanisms involving action plans, output/performance measures;
- statements of how aims are to be targeted or their achievement 'proved';
- examination and re-examination of the use of scarce resources;
- a discussion of priorities;
- flexibility, and the delegation of problem solving and responsibility;
- responsibilities defined in terms of results;
- assessment of staff performance;
- a commitment to making these principles work.

If managers are to pursue keyworking as a 'value for money system', they will have to establish adequate procedures to assess effectiveness. They will need to establish clear goals and targets that consider and project the way the system will operate, and what outcomes are expected from its operation. This may be done at the differing levels of:

1. overall establishment philosophy;
2. general standards and principles of care; and
3. devising and implementing of personalised care plans.

Processes of monitoring and evaluation will need building into the system so that the degree of attainment of such goals and targets can be objectively assessed.

Thus a setting's collective policy and performance review can be largely expressed in terms of the desired outcomes of keyworking. Management and supervision of keyworkers can involve a continual shaping and refining of the performance of individual keyworkers and teams to these targets. The evaluation of effectiveness here can also be a process of checking whether there is an acceptable balance between expectations, accomplishments, and considerations of cost-effectiveness.

Much of this process of individual evaluation and appraisal of a keyworker's performance may be carried out in supervision. Keyworking systems enable a co-ordinated approach to supervision to be carried out. Group supervision through the medium of a task centred discussion of the needs of individual service users or group of users allocated to an individual keyworker can also be used. Lines of responsibility should be made clear here and roles can be similarly defined. The question of who holds case accountability will need addressing and the limits of an individual keyworker's role and tasks clearly laid down, so that conflict over roles is avoided and expectations are clarified. Participative management and teamwork are crucial elements of effective working and decision-making here.

In order to 'make the system work', all parties involved in system design, operation, and processes of intervention and service delivery will need to be involved in decision-making and evaluation. Wherever possible the service user should be placed at the centre of such concern. The use of keyworkers in the enabling of service user based decision-making and in relation to choices in daily living should not be underestimated. In recognising Keyworking as a system that works with the realities of caring practice and service user choice the nature and frameworks of policy formulation and evaluation will involve a variety of different parties and interests.

The setting up (or re-tuning) of any system will involve the talking through of design and principles of operation with the staff and service users involved. The accountability of keyworkers will need talking through in relation to service users and to management. The context of decision-making processes may need to be debated in relation to these areas. It may be useful to consider carefully the rights of keyworkers and service users. Keyworking if it is to be effective must take on board all these issues in the context of the relationships within the staff and the service user team.

A keyworker system can thus be seen as a unified entity in which the analysis of processes and outcomes can be undertaken. The focus here is upon service user choice in daily living. Keyworker systems provide an integrated approach to managerial practice, care planning and the individualisation of care. This perspective naturally lends itself to an ongoing structured approach to value for money issues as part of the normal operation of a setting. The analysis of inputs, the review of systems and processes and the review of policy objectives in relation to output are procedural highlights here. It is the operational clarity that keyworker systems promote that provides the cornerstone for the development of this particular methodology.

STAFF DEVELOPMENT AND SUPPORT

Of key importance to the operation of a keyworker system are supervision, support and training. These enable keyworkers to carry out their tasks effectively. No keyworker system can hope to be really effective unless adequate training is instituted as part of the package. Delegation of authority to keyworkers enables personal development and provides scope for keyworkers to carry out a full range of tasks cultivating their user centred role. Delegation however requires adequate supervision and training if it is to be effective. As we have already stated, the nature of the delegated tasks themselves and the scope of the delegation, will need clear definition.

The career development needs of keyworkers should be part of an overall staff development plan for work settings. Appraisal of performance and development opportunities should form a key element here. There is little point in giving workers additional responsibilities and duties, if these are not monitored and opportunities created to perform well/ develop in these roles. Individual Keyworkers should all be seen as crucial members of the caring team. That team will itself need developing, acknowledging the essential role and function that keyworkers carry out.

SUPERVISION

Clear accountable supervision by managers (in the context of the team) is integral to the success of keyworker schemes in all settings. A positive foundation for supervision is the agreement of keyworkers to the roles, duties and tasks that they will be expected to carry out. A framework for supervision will include:

- clear definition of the responsibilities of keyworkers;
- the degree of their individual accountability;
- the limits of their decision-making powers; and
- their relationship to service users, fellow workers, supervisors and outside agencies.

As Atherton (1986) says, supervision cannot replace good management. It is complementary too it, and requires appropriate structures and practice. The managerial agenda discussed throughout this chapter will need to be carried out if supervision is to be effective. Management will need to define the task and hold the boundaries of keyworking in a general sense throughout the setting.

The supervisor is the link between the keyworker and the wider organisation. They interpret the requirements and make sense of a multitude of professional judgments with the keyworker. The context of care planning is clearly set here in relation to the use of resources, and in relation to accountability for action. The supervisor/keyworker link is thus the direct line for the service user into the organisation itself.

According to Coulshed (1990) and Atherton (1986) supervision is aimed at improving the quality of life for service users. Thus in supervising keyworkers, it is meant to:

- promote professional and personal development;
- provide learning opportunities so as to enhance the quality of work;
- develop and awareness of the keyworker's roles and responsibilities;
- acquire greater understanding of people, problems and situations;
- provide a sounding board for ideas, concerns, plans and strategies;
- build professional competence, creativity and new ways of working;
- give feedback about performance and personal functioning;
- encourage motivation where this may be lacking;
- review and plan work.

Atherton (1986) is clear that the objectives of supervision need to be linked with recognisable outcomes. These should form the basis of a shared agenda between supervisor and keyworker. Such a contract may be made explicit in a written statement about the objectives and topics proposed for supervision sessions. What each party has to do in order to meet these objectives may also be itemised. All these aspects should be expressed in a tangible manner

Kadushin (1976) identified three aspects of supervision:

administrative, educational and supportive. These are clearly mutually interdependent. Whilst they may form the basis of a contract they are also wider, in that the skill of the supervisor is the assessment of contingencies. They determine when it is appropriate to emphasise one aspect more than another in order to achieve the maximum possible motivation and effectiveness of the keyworker.

The administrative/ managerial task in supervision concerns the work and its measurement against qualitative and quantitative standards. It may be considered a positive control that will ensure the translation of caring policies into individual and collective practice. An agreed overall philosophy of the establishment is of contextual importance as the supervisory agenda is worked through. Appraisal of the performance of the keyworker; coordinating, facilitating and sanctioning of their work, and the facilitation of their active participation in the ethos of the establishment are all aspects of this agenda. Thus the administrative task develops and maintains the context of keyworker practices in relation to the overall requirements of the setting.

Supervision of keyworkers has a system maintenance function. It also concerns the creation of an understanding of the process and expected outcomes of individualised service user care. It is a truism to state that the effect of the relationship and the situations that the keyworker becomes involved in are the impacts of significance here. Supervision is thus educative as well as managerial and administrative. These supervisory roles intermingle, yet do need to be understood separately if supervisors are to work effectively.

Supervisors will need to be alert to the dangers of over concentrating upon administrative needs. These can be overcontrolling and promote disabling anxiety. Close supervision is not supervision it is pure direction and inappropriate to the dynamic relationship between the keyworker and service users. The educative function of supervision enables development teaching and learning in relation to the task. It involves learning how to do the job more effectively, and the development of a professional orientation. The content here concerns self awareness, problems solving and discussion of the process of care in relation to care plans and environmental requirements. It is thus about functioning on the job. Whilst this clearly involves discussion of long term goals and the overall sense of direction of service user care it also concerns 'nitty gritty' aspects of caring practice; the problems and issues of the moment. Similarly supervisors may need to recognise that under-control can leave keyworkers uncertain, purposeless and 'open to delinquency'.

The 'teaching content' is the keyworker's opportunity to develop skill. It can be based upon systematic, critical analysis of the keyworker's work that has been carried out and that it is proposed they will carry out. Building and refining areas of strength, addressing blockages and gaps in experience and knowledge.

The third thread is the supportive element of supervision. Keyworkers will have many job- related stresses integral to their caring role. The role of care worker can sap the emotions and can engender feelings of impotency. Workers need to develop attitudes and feelings conducive to the personal relationships that denotes the strength of their work. Supportive supervision is thus concerned with expressive needs of the keyworker.

The demands of the role and the accountability expected for actions inherent within the framework of supervision sessions, demands compliance and performance that may be hard to meet without the necessary professional support, counselling and help. It is not good enough to just appraise keyworkers of the requirements of their role; they also need assistance in the creation of the personal reserves of energy and in the creation of a frame of reference to meet requirements. Central to these needs are the ability to see and work to priorities, the ability to cope with the volume of work and the ability to handle conflicts engendered within the process of meeting individual and group needs in everyday living.

The learning demands of the 'student' role in supervision

when keyed into the stressful nature of the keyworker/user relationship requires the supervisor to assist the keyworker in working through that stress and to avoid potentially damaging failures. The supervisor should be available, approachable and communicate confidence. They should share responsibility for difficult decisions, giving the opportunity for working issues through, helping the keyworker to clarify goals. The supervisor should enable independent functioning and work towards probable success in task achievement.

It is the nature of keyworking with its task focus that in turn creates a task centred focus for supervision. The need for purposeful work, for the delineation of activities and what is to be accomplished sets the basis and rationale for focused supervision.

In many social care settings there is a group element to the task and therefore to supervision. This medium resolves the conflict created by individualisation that is the main danger of keyworking practice. According to Pettes (1979) the administrative, teaching and supportive elements of supervision can be carried out in a group setting with a mandate for implementation in the group and through the group. A task oriented group creates organisational accountability more readily than a collection of individuals. The common interest creates identity, although the leader will need to be aware of individual differences. Peer elements in the supervision process can also be enabled. The team may be used as a tool for staff development where the group training medium is efficient and effective.

Coulshed (1990) develops this theme by suggesting that such a group could discuss ways of improving the quality of their work and exchange ideas. Thus there are major benefits:

- ideas used from everyone (no matter what their position in the organisation) - enhanced creativity and problem solving;
- development of teamwork and team spirit and understanding between keyworkers.

The need for trust and skilled group working on the part of the manager/supervisor is evident.

Kadushin (1976) continues to say that core skills necessary for a supervisor to acquire for both individual and group work include:

- the ability to establish good working relationships based upon rapport;
- listening skills;
- the ability to avoid biases and prejudices particularly in relation to culture;
- the ability to be objective and not allow the emotions to overtake responses; and
- the ability to enable elaboration and clarification.

Goals and targets are of little use if sessions do not challenge, confront issues and offer feedback. Supervision is the reflective soundboard of practice. It will achieve much if based upon a clear sense of the task of keyworking. It should give keyworkers the sense of purpose that is germane to the maximisation of the benefits of any system.

The most effective supervisors stay in role and manage their authority and power in a coherent and professional way. They recognise their own strengths and limitations. They will talk quite explicitly with keyworkers about their needs. They are aware of the 'people management 'aspects of their role and know how different keyworkers respond to differing challenges. What inspires one keyworker will not necessarily do the same for another. Supervision concerns motivation as much as 'good' practice and the individualisation of the framework elaborated here is essential to results.

Coulshed (1990) elaborates the stages in considering content and process of the supervision process (particularly where it focuses upon incidents) in order to achieve these ideals:

- keyworkers should describe situations unhindered by intrusion from the supervisor;
- the supervisor will need to *clarify* the meaning in order to understand the situation;

- *analysis* of helping factors and learning points should be promoted by the supervisor; and
- consideration of the nest step involved and its *implementation*.

Emphatic listening, establishing rapport in the early stages, then widening issues followed by summarising learning points are all aspects of process and technique.

Atherton (1986) promotes analysis in supervision topics of the tension between the elements discussing individual service users, the effect of users on each other and the group aspects of settings. The agenda for a wider basis of supervision that the individual user is essential for keyworker systems to get beyond a tendency to concentrate upon individual rather than community responses to provision. Thus as well as asking questions like 'what are the talents? what are the hopes?' (of the individual service user) issues such as 'what are the norms of the group(s) of users? what kind of leadership is there? How does the group exert pressure on its members? what part does the staff play in creating sub-groups?' need you be opened out and explored.

Supervision is essential to all good keyworker systems not just to the operation of individual keyworkers. I have here endeavoured to elaborate upon the component parts of sound supervision. I have endeavoured to identify the task, framework and requirements of supervisory practice. No keyworker system should be without a complementary supervisory system.

DELEGATION OF AUTHORITY

According to the Industrial Society (Forrest, 1984) delegation is not the same as 'giving out work'. It involves responsibility, authority and accountability.

Thus keyworkers in carrying out their job have the responsibility for the task and the duties involved. The authority to carry this out is delegated by the supervisor. This means the power or right to make decisions and take action in order to enable the responsibility to be discharged. Clarity of the boundaries of this is important, particularly where the responsibility for part or parts of the overall task may be shared between keyworker and supervisor. Accountability means 'carrying the can' for the responsibility: that is being ultimately held to account for the results.

Successful delegation of responsibility will match it to appropriate and reasonable authority and the lines and extent of accountability will also be made clear and will also be reasonable and appropriate (given the nature of the task and the structure of the setting).

Ultimately the manager is accountable. She/he is supervising the work, even though the task in hand is carried out be the keyworker. Hence the importance of appraisal of performance, training for the job and the quality of supervision and relationships involved.

Thus, keyworkers job descriptions need to be clear who is responsible for what aspects of the overall task. The boundaries of this should be stated in writing and the interrelationship between other members of the team and the supervisor made clear. At the stage of setting up a keyworker system a review of such documentation will be required so that it all 'fits' logically together. This will also have to be subject to review when the new system 'beds down'.

EVALUATION TO ACHIEVE QUALITY

Keyworker systems need to have a clear sense of direction and be able to prove effectiveness, in order to maintain standards and develop. An internal quality evaluation system permeates all aspects of the group living experience and its organisation. It concerns processes, shaping and refining performance, striving for continuing improvement, based upon agreed outcomes.

Thus, you should ask yourself whether you are generating evidence to show that agreed outcomes have been achieved and that policies have been put into practice. Do you monitor the use of resources to ensure that they are used to the greatest effect? Have you identified ways of developing and promoting excellence in care practice? Are you identifying structures and processes for effecting improvements in the setting? Are you generating evidence of service users' experience of care?

Managers and staff working with service user's and relatives need to define how philosophies may be achieved. The involvement of users in decision-making can be achieved through a variety of different ways such as an effective users' committee, having users on interviewing panels for new staff posts, having regular group meetings in specific units, or by placing the responsibility upon keyworkers to work on a 'contractual' basis with service users.

If evaluation is to be effective in assessing how well philosophies and objectives have been achieved, you will need to provide for efficient collection of information. This must be reliable, consistent, and valid (e.g. when applied across different units or keyworkers). It must be relevant and practicable: able to measure those aspects most pertinent to effective care. Performance may be targeted relative to objectives in order to promote improvement

Qualitative information is also invaluable, the recording of service users' experience is part of the picture of what is happening. This information should again be obtained systematically and be related to the objectives of the establishment to achieve a clear sense of focus about the task.

From all this information can be highlighted the success of the setting, and also the pressure points of what is not working effectively. The manager's job is to enlist the staff team in finding where problems and weaknesses are, and to enable them to attend to the issues.

Evaluation concerns the making of choices between alternative practices; the validation of policy and practice improvements and the building of a stable foundation for effective practice. Managers and their staff team need to build evaluation strategies into keyworker systems, assessing how well practice and structures stand up to scrutiny.

The process of evaluation starts with setting clear criteria upon which effectiveness may be measured, projecting desirable outcomes before deciding or implementing policy. It then involves assessing why, or how far these criteria have been met.

Feedback is a key requirement of evaluation in order to learn whether the objectives of the keyworker system have been achieved as intended and discovering whether there have been any unintended consequences. It allows informed decision-making and policy review, obtaining information to improve and inform practices and procedures.

Evaluation starting prior to the beginning of implementation of a keyworker system guides implementation. It provides information necessary for programme improvement, modification and management. The focus is on processes and the impact required: the determination of required results and effects of programmes. The aims of evaluation may vary from ensuring compliance with policy to keeping track on the efficiency or effectiveness of keyworking practice. If this is carried out with the staff team in conjunction with service users, it need not be an issue of control; rather it is about enabling and acknowledging good practice.

Thus it could be argued that service users should be a central part of evaluating a keyworker system. In effective keyworking service users are 'better off' as a result of the implementation of the system. Managers and keyworkers alike need to be clear about the outcomes that are desired by service users and how these are to be reviewed. As a particular system is customised to the needs of the service user group and plans are made to meet individual needs, the exercise of service user choice in determining the nature of outcomes is of fundamental importance.

The setting up or re-tuning of any keyworker system should involve talking through its principles with the staff and service users involved. Evaluation with service users requires the continual consideration and reconsideration of the goals and methods for group care and for individualised care.

Such review will lead to a mutually agreed view (between service users and staff) of the nature of the social care task required for the setting, its philosophy of care and of requirements for devising and implementing individual care plans. The mutual understanding required concerns courses of action to achieve specified results. In respecting and enabling user based decision-making, the power imbalance between service users and keyworkers/ managers must be acknowledged. Service users should be enabled to feel that their views and their agreements are appropriate, relevant and will be acted upon.

Performance review of the collective achievement of care philosophies is readily achieved within a methodology that involves a clear definition of outcomes, requirements, goals and philosophies of care. A clear definition of inputs and outputs will promote a sense of clarity in the consideration of effectiveness. Goal displacement will be minimised if managers evaluate the operation of such a system and monitor its effectiveness in a planned way.

Thus the establishment's collective policy and performance review can be partially expressed in terms of a discussion of the service users' desired outcomes. Management and supervision of keyworkers will thus involve a continual shaping and refining of the performance of individual keyworkers and teams to these targets. The evaluation of effectiveness here is also a process of checking whether there is an acceptable balance between expectations, accomplishments, and considerations of cost-effectiveness.

Continued evaluation and review is necessary if effectiveness is to be maintained. Models of system maintenance analyse inputs, conversion processes and outputs. The important question we have posed is the way in which the processes of enabling service user choice through keyworking will begin to shape this review. In managing processes it is important to be clear about inputs and desired outputs so that an understanding can be made of the efficiency and effectiveness of the whole setting. Thus the quality of the processes are judged upon these criteria. The management and supervision of processes here would involve a continual shaping and refining of the performance of individual keyworkers and teams to the agenda set jointly between staff and service users.

Basic questions to pose on review are:

- Do the issues still exist?
- Has there been any deterioration or improvement in the situation?
- Have the desired outcomes of intervention been achieved?
- How effective was the process?
- Is further work required on these issues?

If the desired results have been attained, it is helpful to both keyworkers and service users to consider how this has happened. The service users in particular may build upon this experience of success in developing an ability to become more forceful and independent. Unless it is clear how progress has been achieved, the service users will not be able to generalise it in this way.

Evaluating the extent of change also concerns factors other than the objectives selected in planning exercises. Change and progress may have occurred in other areas and attempts should be made to establish the reasons for this. Progress in one area of difficulty can provide motivation and encouragement for service users and keyworkers to tackle other areas of concern.

Following Isaac and Mitchel (1981) the nature of evaluation in keyworker systems can be represented by the following diagram:

Following Alkin (1971) the process of evaluation of a keyworker system should focus on improvement and development of the system. It starts with an identification of requirements to be fulfilled by the system, exploring any discrepancy between what is and what ought to be. Techniques useful here include brainstorming in user's

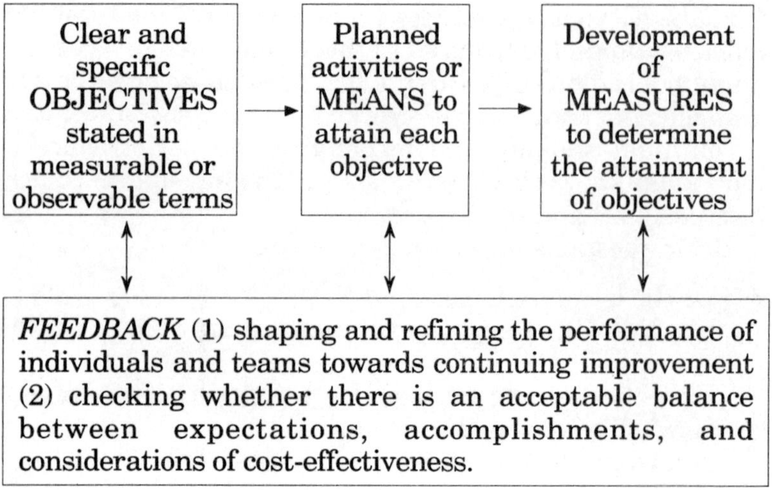

committees and staff meetings. Group sessions may explore strengths and weaknesses.

Requirements teased out by such exercises may be prioritised by service users, keyworkers, and supervisors. Goals for change may then be set. From these specific, measurable objectives are derived and a plan containing the means to attain these objectives formulated. A plan should contain strategies and activities that will be carried out in order to fulfil any changes. Managers and keyworkers may then seek out discrepancies between the plan and reality. The task is to keep the plan true to its design, modifying it as appropriate. Progress towards achieving objectives may then be monitored.

Evaluation is not without its criticisms. It assumes that planning is a rational process which, of course, often breaks down in the practice of keyworking. Aims themselves may conflict or be subject to displacement Policy is assumed to be exactly as described yet there may be a difference between official policy and effected policy. It is also assumed that problems can be solved in a 'scientific' framework and that services are functional rather than the effect of competing interests.

If these issues are to be overcome, all parties (e.g. service users, carers, keyworkers, and supervisors) should be involved in ways that take account of their differing interests. Not only should differing views of success be taken into account, but also how success or failure may be dependent upon different professional and practical criteria.

ACHIEVING A WELL MANAGED KEYWORKER SYSTEM

A checklist for development

Crucial questions should thus be asked by managers if they are to achieve keyworker systems with clear operational guidelines in an enabling management style:

- Has a *firm enabling leadership style* been established by:
  - *Participative working practices*?
  - *Common agreement* on issues?
  - *Democratic style*?
  - *Team support* and *supervision*?
  - *Communication* in *relationships*?
  - *Consultation* within the team to offer *support*?
- Have *variations in quality* between individual keyworkers been tackled?
- Are there *structures to debate* any *differences* of opinion between service users and keyworkers?
- Has adequate *training* of keyworkers to carry out the role been undertaken?
- In providing *24-hour cover* have systems been created to enable others to know the service user?
- Does the process of *matching* create good relationships?
- Are junior personnel given *responsibility*?
- Have the main *roles of supervisors* and quality in fulfilling them been established? Of particular note here are:
  - *Evaluating outcomes*?
  - *Group monitoring*?
  - Enabling keyworkers to give *quality care*?
  - *Training* keyworkers?
  - Fine tuning of *matching*?

  - *Assessment* and *reporting*?
  - *Co-working* and/or cover?
  - *Goal setting*?
  - *Care planning, review*?
  - Attention to *records*?
  - Clarifying with keyworkers *what has to be done*?
  - Taking lead in staff/ keyworker *meetings*?
  - Developing *strategies* to meet *special needs*?
  - Developing *joint contract* with keyworkers?
  - *Review* of *system*?
  - Providing a *point of contact* in absence of keyworker?
  - Giving *feedback* to staff?
  - Maintaining *links* with relatives about decision-making?
  - *Support and development*?
  - Facilitation of *planning*?
  - Maintaining and developing *effectiveness*?
- Does the *management style* enable:
  - *Clear leadership*?
  - *Consultation*?
  - *Positive action*?
  - *Job enrichment*?
  - *Self awareness*?
  - *Positive awareness*?
  - *Staff support* and *development*?
- Does the *quality control* process take into account:
  - *Developing resources*?
  - *Defining staff roles* and *responsibilities*?
  - *Evaluating results*?
  - *Clarifying goals and targets*?
  - Establishing an *agreed basis* for *change*?
  - Frequent *team review*?
  - *Supportive feedback*?
  - Agreement on *evaluation measures*?
  - *Monitoring of delegated task completion*?

- Does the *policy and philosophy of the setting* in relation to keyworking include:
  - *Objectives* that are clear and precise and bear up to analysis?
  - *Role* of the manager?
  - *Defined roles* and *responsibilities* for keyworkers?
  - *Evaluation* of *results*?
  - *Clarification of goals and targets*?

Eight

Co-keyworking

INTRODUCTION

In many situations the duties of keyworkers are shared by pairing, so that decision-making is made in a climate of mutual support and available staff expertise is pooled. The structures and processes involved will determine the quality of teamwork and the overall effectiveness of the keyworker systems involved.

THE NATURE OF CO-KEYWORKING

Research by the author (Mallinson, 1993) in residential care for older people showed that co-keyworking was practised in 47 per cent of establishments with keyworker systems. The details are classified and itemised below in the respondent's own words. These illustrate the variety of forms and methods of co-keyworking.

Co-keyworking based upon hierarchy:

- Senior and junior staff work together.
- Senior staff teach junior staff.

Co-keyworking based upon teams:

- A small establishment, where keyworkers work together.

- Based upon groups of staff and residents.
- Daily discussions in the staff group.
- The staff are divided into two teams.
- The establishment is split into units, staff act together as primary workers in teams.

Co-keyworking based upon formal pairing:

- Two senior carers work together.
- On rota basis staff act across for each other.
- Staff work together in pairs, keyworking for themselves and co-keyworking with a colleague; with joint discussion on a day to day basis.
- 2-5 keyworkers in each care group of 12 service users cover as co-keyworker when the keyworker is not on duty.
- Two keyworkers work together with four service users.
- Staff formally paired as backup workers.
- Two keyworkers work with six service users.
- Each unit has two co-keyworkers, cover absences.

Co-keyworking based upon pragmatic arrangements:

- Holiday and sick cover by staff taking over.
- Some more physically disabled service users require the help of 2 care assistants.

There are many different versions of co-keyworking systems, the variations depend upon the circumstances involved and the aims of the particular system.

ARRANGEMENTS FOR CO-KEYWORKING

When particularly promoting teamwork, staff interaction, communication between staff and service user choice in allocating workers, any given keyworker can be paired with a different colleague for each service user they are responsible for. Thus if a keyworker has six allocated service users, they may then be paired with six other different keyworkers, sharing the responsibility for each user with a different colleague, resulting in six separate pairings (one for each of the six service users.) This model if represented on a chart would seem like a web of service user/keyworker allocations woven around and throughout a residential establishment.

In residential settings that have a number of small living groups, a mini-version of this particular system, operating just within each unit is often used. A less complex version could allocate a pair of workers to a single small group of users, but here the potential for establishment wide discussion of issues throughout the staff group during the normal working day would be lost. There are, of course, many other possible variations.

Some establishments allocate primary responsibility for a particular service user to one keyworker (based upon the preferences of service users) and then allocate a backup (secondary) role to the another keyworker. Here, if an excess of demand for a particular 'primary' keyworker exists, service user choice can be maintained by a preferential allocation to the backup keyworker. The backup keyworker may take a greater responsibility and interest in the service user than they might otherwise have done. The boundaries of responsibility and accountability need to be defined more clearly here then they would within another system.

CO-KEYWORKING PRACTICE

Co-keyworking provides a framework for a greater and more informed debate in care planning, focusing service user needs and decision-making options within the staff team. It enables service users to chose between the value systems represented by different workers. The pairing of keyworkers means that service users have two people to discuss their particular views with and two people with whom to talk through the points involved. Service users can chose to which of the two keyworkers they feel they wish to initially talk to. The workers involved will have to reach agreement on the way forward, debating options between themselves and with the service user.

No one worker may be allowed to impose their own values on a service user without the cross-questioning of their colleague. The worker feeling the strongest about a user's situation, or having particular skills in advocacy may then take a lead in pushing issues forward on the user's behalf. The danger of collusion between workers is a factor to be borne in mind, and one which would have to be considered carefully in staff supervision.

The constraints upon service user choice in the process of matching service users and keyworkers together are considerably modified by co-keyworking. Where traditional systems may fall down in their matching processes due to unbalance in the composition of the staff group, difficulties in fulfilling the wishes of individual service users will not exist to the same degree. For example demands of Black service users to have Black keyworkers, or the demands of female service users for female keyworkers may be overcome. Put simply, one scarce element within the staff group that is in demand may be allocated to twice as many service users when co-keyworking is the system of allocation. Thus users may feel happier about decision-making processes. They may become more involved as there is more scope for ensuring a high degree of compatibility between service user and keyworker. The temptation to allocate Black keyworkers singly to Black service users, causing division amongst staff and service user groups, is avoided.

Co-keyworking allows for sharing between Black and white staff and the development of learning situations through common discussion rather than isolation. Co-keyworking has the potential to increase service user choice by not restricting the service user to the interests of any one worker. Safeguards may need to be considered to avoid the possibility of a small number of keyworkers becoming overloaded with responsibilities and work, whilst others 'escaping' involvement in care planning and in service user contact. It is possible for the workload to be distributed equally amongst the staff so that service users requiring the most attention are allocated to more able staff.

ELIMINATING PROBLEMS IN KEYWORKER SYSTEMS

One of the biggest single problems in keyworking practice is cover for annual leave, sickness, courses etc. With co-keyworking, absences will be less demoralising for staff as well as service users, as the system automatically continues to provide cover in any keyworker's absence. Outside agencies are still able to contact nominated keyworkers through periods of staff leave. Similarly, the ideal of 24hr keyworking cover can become nearer a reality. Should a keyworker leave, during the period that a replacement is sought, keyworking cover can be provided automatically by the existing co-keyworker. New keyworkers would pair up with existing keyworkers who already know the particular service user and are involved in their care planning. Thus co-keyworking systems promote greater continuity in care.

As the system promotes communication and teamwork, keyworkers are less isolated and less immediately dependent upon management for the focus of service user decision-making. Managers may concentrate more upon their primary task of overall monitoring and professional supervision rather than day to day control. Group supervision with its potential for greater teamwork and staff support becomes a more feasible option. Staff will have much more common ground brought about by the sharing of roles.

MUTUAL SUPPORT

Joint discussions by keyworking pairs results in more focused care plans being presented to managers who may have accountability. Thus the discussions may be more meaningful and disagreement between the manager and keyworkers over care plans become less frequent. This may result in a reduction in friction between managers and their staff, enabling a sounder and more rational discussion of decisions and options.

The mutual support that pairs of keyworkers can offer each other in these processes should not be underestimated. Two heads are better than one. The fusing of knowledge and joint development of strategies with service users, debating issues, can become the hallmark of good practice. Keyworkers working in pairs may become more confident in their roles and work. Presentation of material to reviews based upon the observations and professional opinion of *both* keyworkers generally enables a more informed debate to take place. In an enabling managerial climate, constructive criticism of each other, gives pairs of keyworkers a more professional approach to their work and provides a platform to enable service users to develop to their full potential.

Pairs of keyworkers can pool their expertise in working with a particular service user. If written reports present a difficulty to one worker, this may be compensated for by the expertise of their partner. If less able staff are paired with those more skilled, they will be better able to cope with service users needing more intensive tending. Pairing arrangements allow for a certain amount of staff development by the sharing of skills. This must not become a recipe for managerial complacency. Supervision and development of staff is a key part of the managerial role and should continue.

In a well thought out and carefully managed co-keyworking system, staff will work on the basis of sharing roles, thinking through their own strengths and weaknesses. Mutual help and support based upon good communication is essential. The focus will be on debating methods of working and assessing and meeting service user needs. To see such a system merely as allowing two keyworkers a responsibility for one service user is simplistic. It misses the opportunities for good teamwork practice.

SOME PROBLEMS OF CO-KEYWORKING

Co-keyworking will generally enable good teamwork and communication, this is particularly so where these would be already working effectively and are located in a supportive and enabling management style. Where poor teamwork and communication exist, co-keyworking will not meet its goals and will in itself be ineffective. Success breeds success, whereas shortfalls may be exasperated. Establishments already exhibiting poor or ineffective communication and teamwork may find that co-keyworking (with its dependence upon good communication) can breed a downward spiral of ineffectiveness and inefficiency. For co-keyworking to meet service user needs, sound management is essential.

Good management is important to overcome other drawbacks The potential for conflict between pairs of keyworkers is always there. Such conflict if it occurs must be worked through as an absolute priority. The possibility of two workers each pulling in different directions with the service user caught in the middle cannot be discounted. Co-keyworking like traditional forms of keyworking is heavily dependent for success upon coherent philosophies of care shared with and subscribed to by all the staff involved. There is a potential for service user manipulation of keyworkers, or the playing of one keyworker against the other. This is particularly so if there is an element of social control within the role or philosophy of the establishment. This again highlights the need for good communication systems to avoid these pitfalls.

CONCLUSIONS

Co-keyworking provides a viable means to tackle some of the practical drawbacks inherent in the operation of traditional keyworker systems. It can particularly enhance service user choice and allow better staff cover in the event of staff absence. It promotes teamwork and communication, but is dependent upon the quality of these for its efficient operation. Staff development can be enhanced by co-keyworking, but a good enabling management style is required for effective delivery of care. The main drawback of co-keyworking relates to the potential for conflict between pairs of keyworkers. If this occurs it will require good professional supervision to resolve the issues, enabling keyworkers to fully understand the dynamics of the situation that they find themselves in.

Nine

Matching service users and keyworkers

INTRODUCTION

The bringing together of a keyworker and a service user is the initiation of a relationship, the quality of which will determine the effectiveness of personalised care. Successful matching will enable keyworkers and service users to 'get on well' together, providing the foundations for effective keyworking and effective care planning.

A new relationship

According to Butler and Elliott (1985) a new relationship may have many characteristics; excitement, apprehension, relief, cynicism, challenge, adaption, exploration, resentment, and fear. Embarking on a new relationship, service user and keyworker experience these reactions. They have to work through their implications. Thus the process of matching takes into account ways of working through the anticipated feelings of both parties. Openness, honesty, reciprocal responsibility, trust, equality and respect are all qualities of all good partnerships.

FACTORS IN THE CHOICE OF KEYWORKER

The Residential Care Association (RCA, 1978) highlighted a number of variables in the choice of keyworker in residential care:

- The purpose of the placement:
  - the service user's needs;
  - the expected length of stay;
  - the care plan (ie the type of placement and how this reflects needs, and the expected length of stay);
  - the likelihood of rehabilitation or habilitation.
- The previous and current experience of the service user:
  - the established relationships prior to admission and relationships formed early in the placement;
  - the service user's sex, and age; ethnic, cultural and religious factors;
  - the previous experience of the service user, particularly hereditary, genetic and environmental factors;
  - the existing family ties and other external influences.
- The previous and current experience of the worker:
  - the worker's sex, age, cultural, ethnic and religious factors;
  - skills, experience and training;
  - their existing workload and availability;
  - any established relationships between the service user and worker(s).
- The organisational aspects:
  - the sex, age, ethnic, cultural and religious factors of the parties involved;
  - the total resources of the organisation;
  - the existing workloads of staff available;
  - the time factor.

These have formed a useful starting point for practitioners and managers in their discussions with service users. Factors used in matching keyworkers and service users in residential care for older people were reported in research by the author

(Mallinson, 1993). These are given below. The number of establishments (out of a total of 58) where a specific factor was mentioned is given in brackets, together with the percentage of establishments that this represents. The research results were reported in the respondent's own words:

Competence of staff given service user's needs	18 (38%)
Personality and temperament	14 (24%)
including those of both service user and keyworker	*3 (5%)*
Comparability and acceptance of both sides	13 (23%)
Race, colour, creed, culture, language	*7 (12%)*
Time given service user / availability of staff	*7 (12%)*
Attitudes and beliefs	*7 (12%)*
Communication	5 (9%)
Gender	*4 (7%)*
Service user preference	*4 (7%)*
Rapport	*4 (7%)*
Age	*3 (5%)*
Hobbies, and interests	*3 (5%)*
Understanding, and empathy	*2 (3%)*
Background knowledge and home situation awareness	*2 (3%)*
Previous history of service user and keyworker	*2 (3%)*

These appear in many cases to key directly into processes of decision - making. Whilst process is discussed later in this chapter, it is useful to state these research results here. Matching was carried out by:

- compatibilities in personalities and interests;
- more senior workers with more difficult service users;
- gender and mixture of permanent and day care users;
- personality, relationship - fair work load;
- someone with knowledge of service user interests, home area, personality and approach of care assistant needs to be appropriate to service user needs;
- needs of service user, experience/ability of keyworker and ethnic background.

These variables will thus have a considerable significance in any debate between staff and service users about matching. For example, is it appropriate to match male keyworkers with male service users? Many male service users may express a belief that it is not appropriate for them to be bathed by a male: somehow it is 'wrong' and it may contravene their norms. The value systems of some male service users may promote the view that care is women's work. On the other hand, the same service users may feel more comfortable if shaved by a male worker. Cultural and religious norms may also for some service users dictate the sex of the person to whom they are willing to expose their intimate bodily functions. It is only through frank discussion that these kind of elements can be brought into the open and issues resolved.

The early stages of matching will thus involve, in general terms, establishment wide discussion of the significance of these factors. Later, feelings about the significance of all these variables for each individual will need to be aired before a particular matching is agreed.

FEELINGS ABOUT RELATIONSHIPS

Feelings and emotions will form a central part of the proposed relationship. The understanding of each other's behaviour and attitudes has the effect of reducing stress, minimising anxiety and the creating the potential for personal growth.

Negative feelings can be predicted and should talked about openly. Most can be turned around and harnessed positively to establish mutual trust. Past experiences and present feelings all contribute to the emotional overlay of caring practice. Emotions containing elements of irrationality will actively work against establishing positive relationships. These issues will need talking through at the early stages of the matching process. If a relationship subsequently does not work, there may not be anything 'wrong' with the participants, matching will have to be reconsidered however, so that the quality of individualised care can be maintained. The process of matching will need to take place over a considerable period of time for these aspects to be considered.

Taking the significance of ethnicity or 'race' in matching keyworkers and service users as an example, an understanding may be gained of the importance of beginnings.

Racism is a white person's problem and should be seen as an issue for white people. An invalidation and exploitation of black people is unfortunately ingrained in the white consciousness. Despite a genuine concern by many white people, it is unlikely that they can really know the pain and the suffering which people of different cultures and skin colour have endured and continue to endure. Racism is disabling and devalues relationships.

Thus, the question of whether a white service user should be placed with a black keyworker may depend upon each person's perception of the proposed relationship. A Black worker will need to feel that they can develop and give of themselves. Issues should be explored openly and sensitively. Feelings about a white person, that is questions of respect, and trust can provide a basis for working through pitfalls in the making of a relationship. Indeed, the positive sharing of feelings can help modify behaviour and attitudes. In this context, Black keyworkers will value the support of other Black workers in establishing strategies to sensitively challenge and work through possible racism. The manager's task is enable such support systems to develop. Openly discussing these issues will strengthen the anti- racist struggle in a unit. Anti-racism can result in a strong and healthy challenge within a relationship, thus establishing mutual respect.

For most white service users, these issues when explored will strengthen relationships. However if a service user openly makes racist statements the situation will need appropriately challenging by the manager and careful working through, to avoid setting up relationships that will fail. Overt racism from service users should be regarded as unacceptable as overt violence. In some cases it may be appropriate to avoid particular matchings entirely. Managers will also need to act in any instances where relationships have been compromised, so that the quality of care is maintained and so that keyworker job satisfaction is achieved.

A Black service user (like any other person) will need to fully benefit from being in a particular keyworker's care. A judgment has thus to be made about issues in the quality of a prospective matching of a white worker with a Black service user and what will need working through during the matching process. Any possible gaps in the relationship will need working on in the same way as in any other situation. Racism if it occurs will need to be strongly challenged by the manager as a matter of extreme urgency and solutions found that address issues such as the quality of individualised care, prevent recurrence and seek to resolve any pain caused.

In many cases it may be appropriate to match people of the same culture. The overlay of emotion and the commonality of interest and experience can help relationships. For example, a particular keyworker may have knowledge of a minority language that is the only tongue of the service user. The danger of segregation in some establishments should however be borne in mind. The use of language and culture can, however in some situations be crude and unhelpful. A poignant example here is the case of the Polish care assistant 'matched' with the Polish service user: because of the inaccurate assumption made by the manager about the total commonality of language in Poland, they could only communicate with each other in English!

ROLES OF KEYWORKERS

The role a keyworker is to take with a particular individual should be considered as a matter of course. SCA (1988) outlined the main social care roles. Amongst those particularly applicable to keyworking were:

- diagnosis of problems, needs and behaviours;
- planning;
- counselling;
- attitude or behaviour changing;
- directing plans;
- acting as agent on behalf of a service user;
- enabling;
- advocating;
- mediating; and
- support giving.

In meeting service user's needs it has to be asked which roles are appropriate to a particular service user and their care plan; and which are within the repertoire and style of a particular keyworker.

PROCESSES

The process of matching follows no hard prescription. The methods in residential care for older people reported in research by the author (Mallinson, 1993) are given below. These were reported in the respondent's own words. In some cases the interpretation of the author is also given in brackets. Matching is carried out by:

- mutual agreement and observation;
- discussion and negotiation with parties concerned who then decide;
- temperament and suitability - user choice where possible;
- assessment and reviews of specific service user requests, and trying to accommodate;
- discussion with staff member and service user's views;
- temporary /trial allocation;
- staff completing a users and staff relation form/service user choice of likes and dislikes plus ensuring a balanced workload;
- who gets doing things with whom;
- random selection;
- formalisation of existing relationships;

- availability of keyworker;
- allocation of empty spaces;
- trial and error;
- geography of building (i.e. presumably by aspects such as living units);
- vacancy takes next referral:
  - compatibility and vacancy.

Service user and staff may have particular feelings concerning whom they 'get on well with'. An adequate matching system will have a mechanism, agreed by all concerned, to arbitrate in the inevitable situations where one keyworker is extremely popular, having the bulk of service users wishing to be allocated to them. Similarly where one member of staff appears very unpopular, and has few or no service users expressing a preference for them. Some systems may however allow for different sizes of workload. Thus in some circumstances, other team functions may be taken on board in lieu of keyworking responsibilities. An acknowledgement that some staff may have particular strengths in areas other than keyworking may be helpful to enable this and to build a flexible system that enables teamwork and job satisfaction. Other duties include menu planning, and administration of laundry.

Techniques such as questionnaires involving staff and service users may provide initial information that can establish the state of play, narrow down options and establish areas that can be worked through. Examples of questions that staff could be asked are:

- What areas of work are you best at?
- Which tasks do you particularly enjoy doing?
- Which service users do you 'get on' well with?

Examples of questions that service users could be asked are:

- What do you want from your keyworker?
- Which particular staff members do you 'get on' well with?

and so on...

The involvement of staff in discussions with service users during, or after administration of a questionnaire, is desirable. Working through the issues should take place openly and with a sense of both purpose, and sensitivity to the feelings of the people involved.

If logical and clear boundaries can be created in an establishment (for example by small group living) these will narrow down options so that they become more manageable The initial decision may become not so much 'Who is to be my keyworker?' as 'Whom will be my companions in daily living?'

Some workers may have particular specialist knowledge and skills e.g. in working with hearing impaired people, visually impaired service users, or school leavers. These skills can be harnessed by linking known needs with known skills. Another possibility may be an initial grouping by geographical locality of origin.

At the end of the day, there should be established an understanding of how decisions have been realised by all involved and how debates over conflicting interests have been resolved. The use of joint working parties of representative service users and staff, or service user's committees to discuss process and principles is invaluable. Executive decision-making on the final allocation can only be carried out if the broad principles have been already established. People will need to be consulted, and have gained a clear understanding of the constraints involved and their implications. A high degree of overall trust and understanding needs to be established throughout the unit.

Whilst it is important to get it right first time, trial periods may be appropriate, together with the means to change keyworkers. Similar considerations also apply to keyworkers coming new into existing systems, and for new assessments. The pre-admission involvement of possible keyworker(s) needs to build up the sense of trust and establish working relationships. The introduction of any system should have regular formal reviews built in so that problems such as these can be raised and addressed.

CONCLUSIONS

The matching of keyworkers is not an end in itself, it marks the beginning of a relationship which determines the quality of practice and the quality of life. The issues and principles of matching need working through in settings before choices are made. The sense of trust, honesty, mutual respect and accountability that are the highlights of keyworking should be conveyed from the very beginning.

Ten

Implementation in an establishment

INTRODUCTION

Moving into keyworking involves the management of change. Crucial to successful implementation of change is the creation of a climate in which ways of working can be transformed. Staff also need to be involved in devising the new system, so that with total commitment it will be made to work by them. This chapter is an amalgam of the experience of two establishments that each went through such change (on a similar basis). The issues involved are thus brought out into the open and fully discussed based in the reality of the circumstances, and yet full confidentiality is also maintained.

A METHODOLOGY FOR IMPLEMENTATION

When the issue of keyworking was first raised as a possibility within the establishment, it was proposed to staff that the resolving of questions of feasibility, design and implementation should be carried out by a 'task group' composed of a representative group of all staff. Thus most of the discussion regarding the basis of the new system and the negotiation with those involved, would be carried out by the staff themselves with the support and guidance of management.

This decision was based upon an understanding of the positive reasons for adopting a team approach: working towards shared goals, the sharing of values and the generation of commitment. The attitudes and feelings of staff towards keyworking were an element that had the potential to determine the success or failure of the system. Implementation of this approach was carried out after consultation and negotiation with the whole staff. Staff and management together decided the task group's remit and how it should proceed. The involvement of staff in decision-making was in itself seen as promoting the objectives and the philosophy of keyworking.

The staff wished to see a better service for users. The personalisation of care was their goal. Service users could have their physical, personal and emotional needs catered for as the result of giving these specific responsibilities to one 'special' member of staff for each group of service users. This person responsible for the personalisation of their care would be someone who was particularly interested in them. Someone they would be able to talk to, helping in any problems they may have.

The management hoped to increase the interest shown by staff in their work (thus improving job satisfaction, motivation and commitment). For all staff they hoped to establish and identify an improved system of responsibility and accountability. A keyworker system would also help in other problem areas such as the laundry, bathing and the social aspects of care.

The present situation contrasted with that when the home had first opened. At that time, only two service users were said to be incontinent; less than twelve needed any real degree of staff attention. Many service users had been able to go out shopping attend concerts and socials and visit relatives. Now ten years later, with no extra staff, many more service users required physical care. Staff were forced to concentrate upon routine, heavy and task centred work. There was little time to spend upon social and intellectual activity and so service users were becoming bored, apathetic and institutionalised. It was essential to make the best use of staff; they were a very scarce resource.

Staff found it difficult to spread themselves equally around fifty service users. If they were each given specific responsibility for only five service users they would give much more care and attention to those five, having only limited responsibility for the other forty five. This would ensure that all service users had the concentrated attention of one member of staff, rather than the minimal attention of all of them.

THE MANAGEMENT OF CHANGE

The task group clearly saw its primary role as the management of change. Although the objectives involved and their implications were relatively clear, many adjustments in behaviour and previous well established ways of working would be required. The 'human' aspects of change could not be minimised, all aspects of change had to be assessed in terms of the effect upon the individuals and groups involved. The task group thus provided a forum for sharing ideas, suggestions and feelings about the proposed changes. We worked to the principle that total involvement of staff would bring total commitment to the new system and its objectives.

The group promoted the view, to the staff as a whole, that a better service to users would result from keyworking, based upon improved staff/user relationships and increased communication. Opportunities for personal development would also be available to staff. Increased job satisfaction and regular support were all aspects of practice that would need addressing.

We examined Pincus and Minahan (1973) they suggested a number of areas which form a suitable way of viewing change. The first was the system built around the person enabling planned change (or 'change agent' to use their American terminology). This was the role the group was specifically taking upon itself by planning, introducing and implementing the keyworker system.

The second was that of the service user themselves. Pincus and Minahan in highlighting that the user must be the expected beneficiary, suggest that they are only service users in a true sense if they are party to a working agreement or contract. Thus we needed to obtain that agreement. We needed to be sure that this was a change that they wanted. We needed to consult with them and explain the proposed system to them.

The third was that required to change (the 'target' system). In this case it was the care staff that were not on the planning group. They would need to know what goals we were trying to accomplish and how their work would alter in order to achieve these. We needed to involve them in the change process itself so that it did not seem threatening and so that they would not pursue a natural inclination to resist it.

The last area to consider was the effort in changing itself. In discussing the 'action system', Pincus and Minahan suggest that change is only made through other people. Thus they have to be involved. The action system embraced all those involved in efforts to accomplish the task we had set. For example, we needed to involve the senior staff to identify and establish goals. They would be needed to help us obtain a working agreement with the service users and in my working with care staff as the major 'target' of change.

The management team also floated ideas. Key issues here were the part that staff supervision would play in the future system and the responsibilities of keyworkers. Members of the task group and management held meetings with care staff so that feelings, uncertainties, likes and dislikes could be openly expressed. To facilitate this a number of questionnaires on issues and feelings were distributed to staff by the group to encourage them to think and commit themselves to the ideas of the task group. This was to test the wider acceptance of their ideas and to feed the feelings of the staff as a whole into the planning process. The ideas behind keyworking were discussed with ancillary staff and service users. Any suggestions, ideas and feelings were drawn into the debate.

Issues that the task group grappled with included the accountability and responsibility of keyworkers; the methods of individualising care plans and the roles and tasks of the keyworker. The group felt that clear guidelines needed to be drawn up and objectives shared between all staff so that the system could operate coherently and flexibly. These guidelines were drafted jointly by management and by the group.

The task group found that change is a slow an painful process. Davis (1982) indicates that those who initiate it can expect to attract hostility. Those who are required to change face the rejection of their cherished routines and will have their previous strengths challenged and their practices replaced. The group needed reassurance from management about the usefulness of their task. The staff needed leading through the personal and institutional disruption that had to take place. When the motivation for change began to wane, the task group had to develop further responses and generate ideas concerning new situations.

The partnership between management and the task group was important. Careful planning, and the use of supervision and training opportunities to ease the uncertainties and powerlessness felt by the staff as a whole were key elements. Careful preparation had to be made at all levels and with all involved (team manager, officer team, service users and staff). The new system had to be implemented decisively and had to incorporate support and supervision to make it (and the transitional period) work.

The fortnightly task group meetings were based upon the principles of teamwork. All the persons in the group had individual expertise; they pooled knowledge and experience. To be effective, the team had to state views, differences of opinion, interests and problems in an open climate. Issues had to be confronted rather than avoided. The atmosphere engendered was one of trust and rapport.

The group throughout had discussions with individual service users and groups of service users. The need to build upon the service user's feelings about the new system and work through the changes with them was very apparent. Issues that had to be worked through here were how the role of the keyworker would affect service users and who they would be allocated too. Issues were also talked through with groups of staff and service users together.

THE BASIS OF THE SYSTEM

The management and the task group floated ideas jointly. These included the basis of the new arrangements for supervision. The role of supervisor was felt to be an enabler. The need to build up an effective working relationship between supervisor and staff member was clear. Adequate time would be required to help staff develop and implement care plans and to guide them through the emotional demands made by the service user worker relationship. A 'task centred' approach to supervision appeared to be the best way forward. This would enable both parties to clarify their role, to establish clear objectives and to set priorities. A precise, goal orientated approach would enable the encouragement of planned, purposeful work and would help to make accountability clear. The staff group agreed that supervision would be held monthly, with the opportunity for informal contact or additional sessions between these.

The basis of care planning was also considered. Of importance here was the advocacy role of keyworkers. Physical, social, emotional, cultural and intellectual needs could be more easily identified and assessed by the keyworker. These would be reviewed by service user, keyworker and supervisors acting together. In enabling service users to set their own goals, the principles of choice in daily living and the breaking of the cycle of dependency were foremost on our agenda. An aspect of the keyworkers role would be to formulate networks of care as such plans were implemented.

Another major issue to be resolved by the group was the matching of service users and keyworkers. The service user's situation was considered first, for example:

- personal details;
- the reason for reception into care;
- acceptability of individual care staff to the service user;
- previous life experience of the service user including their likes and dislikes;
- race and gender;
- kinds of care plans and care skills that may be required;
- family details and other external factors.

Into these were keyed the nature of the care staff themselves:

- their personal details (including ethnic origin and sex);
- training;
- experience and abilities;
- workload factors such as time; and
- the relationship between staff and staff/users.

A number of general aspects were also considered:

- the broad workload of all staff;
- the total resources available;
- the amount of time care would take;
- agency policies and procedures; and
- the requirements of the formal supervision structure.

The possibilities arising out of all these factors were discussed with groups of service users and staff before a draft (and then later a final list) of service users and their keyworkers was published.

IMPLEMENTATION

As the task group's work proceeded, enthusiasm to see the new system implemented gradually took over. Care staff became easily influenced and persuaded but this was based upon a clear understanding of the required outcomes of cooperation, consistency and continuity of care. The new system was eventually implemented a month earlier than the projected time. This was due partly to the keenness and interest of staff and partly because of a recognition of the need for revised timings that would bring the system well 'on line' before the Christmas period.

We had been surprised that care staff had expressed a wish to work with service users needing the most physical care. This did show commitment to making the system work. Keyworkers saw the most positive aspects of the job to be working with the personality and character of the service users rather than the degree of work involved. Service users had been very anxious to know who 'their own' keyworker was to be. They had been reluctant however to request a particular member of staff.

The first six weeks were taken up by staff making themselves known to service users and their relatives, together with the more physical aspects of care such as bathing, laundry and personal services. Keyworkers made enquiries to find out as much information as they could about their particular service users. There even developed a kind of competition to see how well individual service users were cared for. The general consensus was that the new system was already better than the one it replaced.

The second round of supervision sessions seemed to concern themselves with practical problems such as service users needing new clothes and issues such as service users refusing baths. Keyworkers were coping well with practical aspects of care but needed encouragement to include such things as social and emotional care. They needed pushing to find out how service users felt about things in general and themselves in particular. It was perhaps the better organisation which now brought the physical aspects of service user care into the fore. This was of course the area that staff felt most comfortable with. Perhaps some of the service users found it strange to be talking about feelings and were thus naturally reticent. These issues highlighted the importance of supervision.

After eight weeks there were obvious benefits from the new system. Keyworkers could be seen sitting and talking to service users more often. Letters were being written to friends and relatives on service users' behalf; knitting was being carried out by several ladies; newspapers and magazines were being bought; more ladies were using the hairdressing facility and there was a big increase in the involvement of relatives and staff.

There were also fewer problems with laundry, there were more requests for clothes and services for service users. There were more requests from staff for training. As it was Christmas time the keyworkers decided that they were responsible for buying service users' presents. This was a great deal easier for the officer in charge, but also the service users got more choice. Nobody had to buy more than five presents, previously the officer in charge had to buy fifty! Senior staff now learnt much more about individual service users as they were discussed in supervision sessions.

We checked out with relatives and with individual service users how they felt about the new ways of working. There was a general consensus that things had much improved. Service users in particular now enjoyed having 'a little chat with members of staff'. Ragg (1977) comments that by adopting a personal approach the care worker is able to make a positive contribution to the service user's sense of being and individual person. Individualisation contributes to a person's sense of identity by enriching it and relating the past to the present.

After ten weeks we decided to hold a number of meetings based upon individual shifts and members of the task group. These would share our feelings of progress and also discuss the few small problems that had begun to show up. The main one of these was the general responsibility that keyworkers had for service users *not* on their particular list.

EVALUATION OF CHANGE

As the group evaluated the changes, we realised the importance of consultation in order to achieve effectiveness. Important issues such as confidentiality, decision-making, responsibility and accountability had been best discussed by the staff group. Staff felt that they had been directly involved in introducing the new system and had an understanding of their role within it. They were aware of what was being done, why it was being done and the results that were expected.

There was no lack of evidence to show that the personalisation of care was having its effect. For example, one often overheard service user's remarks, 'I am waiting for Iris, I have a letter from my son to show her', or 'Do you like my nail varnish? Jane bought me some', or 'Mary has asked me to help her make a blanket, I used to do a lot of knitting.' Personalisation of care was dependent upon keyworkers themselves. From the start they showed interest, and attended all the meetings. The extensive preparation had also played a large part, giving staff the understanding, confidence, incentive and enthusiasm. This was illustrated by the fact that they asked to start a week earlier than we had planned.

When discussing value systems in homes, Hudson (1981) says that to get committed staff one first needs something that they feel is worth committing themselves to. One then has to provide a system in which commitment can develop. One must be clear about the task of the home. We feel that the keyworker system provided a framework for achieving all of these. The keyworker is the service user's personal counsellor and the relationship between service user and keyworker must remain alive and purposeful. This set us the first of many long term goals as we maintained and developed our keyworking practice.

We thought in retrospect that there had been a tendency for keyworkers and management to concentrate upon physical care to the detriment of service users' emotional needs. We later began to move towards meeting the social, cultural and intellectual needs of service users. To do this keyworkers had to acquaint themselves with the service users' past as well as the present. This further increased our involvement with relatives and friends. Researching service users' past life history became an essential and also very interesting part of the keyworker's task. Finding details of previous work, hobbies, interests, families, communities and life styles were all part of this. Reminiscence therapy proved to be an effective source of this material. This provided a rich fount of information upon which to base appropriate care planning. Managers were now inundated with requests by staff for resources and facilities so that service users could continue their hobbies. Requests were made for art and craft materials, music, reading and writing facilities and specialist magazines.

The emotional care of service users was more of a challenge. It was an area which was approached with caution and developed more slowly, as feelings were more difficult to cope with than with tasks. Caring for emotional needs became a two way process between keyworkers and service users. It was more demanding of the commitment of keyworkers. As relationships developed and deepened, so did the distress level amongst keyworkers when bereavement or the prospect of bereavement was involved. The supervision and support of staff was crucial.

The issues involved had to be resolved in supervision, or keyworkers would not be able to commit themselves to their next service user. Formal and informal supervision techniques were used. The senior staff supervising had to develop new skills as demands were made upon them. We had to negotiate a training course within the department to meet these needs. The format of supervision sessions moved over time from the discussion of service user's needs to staff needs, so that staff could adequately cope with the demands that emotional care required.

Other issues we had to address ourselves to were, support for service users when a keyworker left and co-keyworking to cover for key worker absence. (The latter was carried out by improving teamwork and making better use of relief staff.)

CONCLUSIONS

Keyworking is now part of our mainstream practice and is an integral part of the style and method of working in the establishment. It is our belief that these changes were made to the benefit of all concerned.

The vision of a new life for the establishment, that had been formulated by the task group was fully realised. The success of this particular keyworker system had clearly been dependent upon staff involvement. They had been motivated to make it work, to enable the benefits to be translated into realities rather than to remain a set of proposals.

The feeling of the care staff was that the task group had helped to get them involved and enabled them to obtain a clear understanding of the issues. The group itself formed a useful staff development exercise. Its remit finished as the changes were evaluated but it provided a model to tackle other issues in the establishment. As a way of managing change we can thoroughly recommend it.

SOME QUESTIONS CONSIDERED BY THE TASK GROUP ON SETTING UP THE KEYWORKER SYSTEM

- What are the roles that keyworkers will undertake?
- What training will keyworkers need to fulfil their new roles?
- How many service users will be allocated to each keyworker?
- How are keyworkers and service users to be matched?
- How are the cultural needs of service users to be met?
- How is the tension between individual care and group living to be resolved?
- Will keyworkers work together in pairs (co-keyworking) to provide cover and mutual support?
- How are keyworkers to be supervised? What methods will be used?
- Who is to be accountable for the care plan (keyworker or supervisor)?
- How are keyworkers to be supported within the team?
- How is the keyworker system to be monitored and reviewed?

Section Three:

Keyworking in Practice – Examples

Eleven

Keyworking in an establishment for older people

INTRODUCTION

This chapter is a portrait of an establishment with a keyworker system. It shows the strengths and weaknesses of the particular establishment. It is illustrates the diversity of approaches to keyworking in residential care as many of the elements here could have appeared in differing forms. There are many individual idiosyncrasies in the approach that this particular establishment takes. It does not necessarily conform to a stereotypical view of what a keyworker system may look like.

This establishment illustrates of one of many ways that some of the issues explored in this book may be tackled. It is included to make the idea of a systems approach to keyworking in residential care tangible. It is based upon a 'real life' establishment although some of the elements of the system have been altered for reasons of confidentiality.

PEN PICTURE OF THE ESTABLISHMENT

The establishment that this chapter is loosely based upon is in the private sector and has 25 service users (4 male, 21 female) all white. It has 3 day care places and offers respite care as available. It is organised into 3 living groups each of approximately 8 service users.

There are 23 full time members in the staff group including domestic staff. Two are male and six are black. In addition there are 10 part time staff (all female of whom 2 are black).

The establishment has statements of aims and objectives in the forms of a prospectus, a charter of rights and a policy document that is used for discussion and supervision.

The establishment makes arrangements for individual care planning through review meetings, contracts / agreements, decision - making shared between service users, relatives/friends and staff, and by goal setting formulated by staff and service users working together.

There is a regular service users' committee (meeting at least once per month), regular staff / service users meetings (meeting at least once per month), regular reviews (occurring at least every six months) and regular day to day informal involvement of service users in decisions.

Keyworkers undertake a variety of tasks. These are listed below in order of importance. One service user only is generally allocated to each keyworker:

1. sitting and listening to service user's joys and worries;
2. admissions;
3. assessment of service users;
4. advocating service user's needs;
5. physical care;
6. counselling;
7. recording;
8. supporting daily living;
9. arranging individual outings;
10. arranging activities.

Keyworkers are supervised on a daily basis by direction of day to day activities; review of job responsibilities and discussion of the service user's care plan.

Service users and keyworkers are matched by personality, disability, age and sex.

Keyworkers have regular contact (i.e. at least once every two months) with:

General practitioners
District nurses
Chiropodists
Religious leaders
Solicitors and family of service users.

Co-keyworking is practised on a rota basis with keyworkers acting across for each other.

The keyworker system is reviewed and monitored through supervision sessions.

In the view of the manager of the establishment, keyworker systems improve personalised care by giving an 'interest to the keyworker'. Relationships are 'like an extended family' whilst 'staff are aware of their responsibility and their aims and objectives. The keyworker is able to keep family and relatives up to date, write letters etc. arrange birthday parties, and send cards to relatives on the service user's behalf'.

THE BASIS OF THE SYSTEM

The official *aims* of keyworking are said to be: to develop relationships, to provide a personalised and responsive service as users require and to make the home a happy place, and service users content.

The system is *managed* by establishing accountability via consultative delegation and a 'corporate responsibility'. The management structure could be said to be organic in that there is:

- a contributive common task;
- individual tasks are set by the concern as a whole;
- a network structure of control and communication exists;
- an emphasis is placed upon lateral communication; and
- upon a notion of primary overall responsibility.

Standards are said to come from the top. Junior personnel

are given responsibility and good morale is said to be the result.

All staff, no matter what their position are *designated as keyworkers* (i.e. management, housekeeping, care staff etc.) They are *supervised* informally (as appropriate) by the Director of Care or another member of the Management Team.

The *role of the supervisor* is to enable staff to give quality care and to train staff in the way the establishment works. If needed supervisors will work in tandem with keyworkers and act as a 'go between' on important issues: making clear with/to staff what has to be done and to check on outcomes. In going though this process they set goals with keyworkers focusing upon the care plan and the keyworker's role as the coordinator of this. They also develop strategies with keyworkers to meet special needs and develop a joint contract concerning ways of working. In doing this they give feedback to staff and maintain links with relatives regarding decision-making. Supervision is said by the staff to create accountability 'if not you know about it...one is clear what has to be done...the follow up with staff is good'.

The main *roles of keyworkers* are to discuss issues with service users, make meaningful recordings, carry out assessments, and manage the care plan with their supervisor. They will also coordinate and review action in order to make things happen in a desirable manner. They will specifically see the service user if they are not happy regarding anything, and see if the service user has a problem and talk about it in confidence. It is their particular job to organise outings for the service user and to always welcome family members and make them feel at home. They will prioritise tasks in discussion with colleagues manager, user and family and involve the family, looking after the service user as if they were a member of the family. Keyworkers will work with the family on weekly basis to deal with problems and obtain agreement on special needs.

In carrying out their *tasks* the keyworker will prioritise requirements by negotiation with the service user (e.g. the timing of serving of drinks). They carry out particular tasks for service user with their agreement. They share in service user's life space by reading, talking and listening, sharing interests and encouraging activities.

Twnety-four hour cover is maintained within the keyworker system by keyworkers substituting in role: any member of unit will step into a keyworker's role if they are absent. The management team is always available to provide backup. Primary carers cover each other. Records and messages are made with a particular focus in mind to ensure continuity and to communicate day to day needs.

Matching of service users and keyworkers is carried out by a creative development of relationships which are later formalised. Service user choice is maintained. Factors in the decision are shared interests depend upon service user's abilities and particular needs. The Head of Care negotiates and formalises the decision.

Relationships are said to be the most important factor in the keyworker system. Typically a keyworker talking about their relationship with service users stated: 'They have a joke, a chat and a moan, it differs every night. I share interests with them, for example, sharing family events and stories from the past.' Another keyworker stated: 'I need to be adaptable and understanding. My role is to enable comfort and security'. Similarly a service user said: 'staff are often under pressure there may not be much time to sit and talk but when they do I am thankful. If I need to make my needs known I will ask the keyworker who will ask for things that a resident cannot. It is the keyworker 'that gets things going'. Expectations are based upon mutual trust.

The *statements of policy* set expectations especially on induction and in the early days of staff employment. They are referred to in supervision if necessary and may be actively used if a problem.

In *care planning* needs are initially examined by the keyworker with their supervisor and with the Director of Care and service user to decide what is to be done. This tends to take the form of day to day discussions and may involve other persons such as relatives. These arrangements are then formalised in forums like reviews with relatives and other professionals. The role of the keyworker here is to advocate ways of meeting needs on behalf of the service user and to produce a report for the review meeting. Thus joint work is undertaken by the keyworker and their supervisor to interpret and advocate the service user's wishes. It is felt that keyworking is fundamental here in assessment getting beyond what would otherwise tend to be a concentration on physical care in planning and meeting needs. Relationships are said to frame the quality of analysis of needs; the keyworker needs to know the service user well. The task of care planning is clear within the framework of the keyworker system. Keyworking is accountable practice.

Decision-making on everyday matters will tend to be done by the supervisor in consultation with the keyworker. Generally speaking, there is a chain of communication on issues being raised with those involved (although on a minor issue such as new clothing the keyworker will tend to deal with relatives direct):

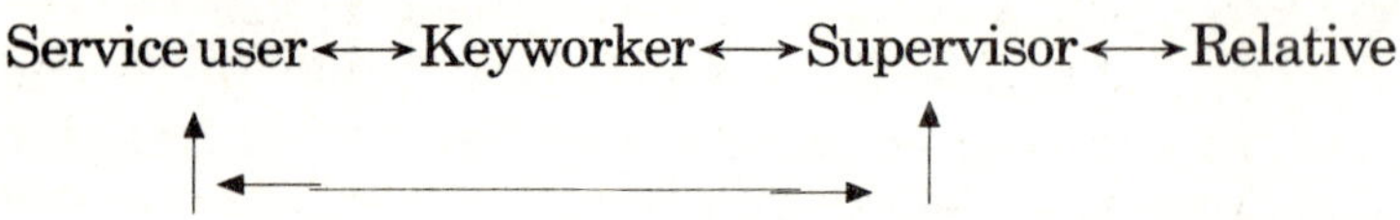

The keyworker system itself is *reviewed* by a proactive stance being taken by supervisors as a group who will 'step in if necessary. The supervision sessions are a useful means to collect and disseminate information here. A 'tight' rein kept informally on the system by the Director of Care. Staff meetings are held to highlight issues and to strive to achieve solutions.

THE EFFECT OF THE SYSTEM

The particular benefits to service users and their relatives are said to be that empathy and tolerance are exhibited.

Keyworkers provide that 'little bit extra' and 'things are done that need to be done'. They are accountable, 'you know where the buck stops'.

Keyworkers who have experienced different ways of working say that they are now more knowledgeable about different service users. Comfort and security are enabled via homely relationships, they get to know service users better 'by living with them' and they will work as a community: as they are 'one of the family'.

Disadvantages of present practice are however said to be variations in level of service, differing objectives and targets and an isolation of keyworkers from the main team It was of significance that those who feel isolated from the team either work nights or were not in 'mainstream' care roles.

CONCLUSIONS

This keyworker system is an effective means of organising care that takes individual needs into account whilst orientating to the requirements of the group. The particular form that this system takes works well in the particular ethos involved and with the particular staff and service user group. The location and the geography of the building also lends itself to this particular form of keyworking.

It is clear that each establishment and the people involved (service users, staff and relatives) should consider the particular approach that will suit them and their needs. They should consider how this varies from other people's practice, rather than slavishly following fixed ideas. The debate amongst the group as to the nature of the system is as important as the actual design of that system. There are however general principles that help to guide and structure practice. This example fits most of the aspects discussed in this book; another establishment down the road could be different yet similarly follow the general principles involved. As a particular example this establishment provides many ideas for debate and many starting points in designing new systems or evaluating existing ones.

Twelve

Interdisciplinary teamwork in residential special education

INTRODUCTION

Social Care and Education are complementary experiences which together mould children into the adults of the future. In residential special education the dual focus of education and social care create mutually inter – dependent roles. Cooperation based upon equality to establish a team approach is vital in meeting children's needs effectively.

Most of the available evidence appears to indicate that where teachers have dominated decision-making, residential special education has in general terms become the poor relation of social care. Social needs may be marginalised in favour of 'educational needs'. This is despite the greater part of the child's day being spent away from the classroom setting. The rationale of residential provision is based upon group living and the development of social competence. Mutual respect, teamwork and the sharing of professional perspectives creates a climate of joint working together to meet the needs of children holistically.

It is upon this professional inter-dependence that the case

for co-keyworking in special education settings, by deliberate pairing of individual social care workers and teachers, is made. This is dependent for its effectiveness upon equal power in decision-making within a climate of mutual support. Staff expertise may be pooled, creating a unified professional perspective. This chapter moves away from existing as separate system partners to the development of new working situations that recognise each other's realities. The focus is upon joint working together to individualise provision.

PROCESSES OF CO-KEYWORKING

In co-keyworking, teachers and care workers need to think through their own joint strengths and weaknesses. The paring of each child with a primary worker from the care side of the school and the appropriate classroom teacher enables a composite assessment of need. It creates a full examination of the child in their everyday environment and a unified approach to care and educational case planning. To see such a system merely as a care worker and a teacher having the joint responsibility for one child is simplistic and misses the opportunities for good teamwork practice.

It is important that roles are clearly and accurately defined. Teachers have a responsibility for formal classroom education; social care staff have a responsibility for the non-classroom based development of the child. The social care task and the teaching task, although separate, must dovetail together. The care worker should have the same delegated degree of responsibility and autonomy for their own practice as has the teacher in the classroom. They are the 'expert' and manager of the care setting: of group living and overall planning for the setting. The boundaries of responsibility and accountability need making clear. Co-keyworking involves the fusing of decision-making structures in planning ways an individual child's needs are to be met. Joint approaches to meeting needs may be defined. These are based upon the separate responsibilities of care and teaching staff in care and classroom provision.

A clear sense of purpose is required for co-keyworking to be effective. Philosophies of care and education must be set out in agreed statements defined by all involved. Co-keyworkers will then work with a clear brief, in the knowledge of the way their individual work fits into the context of the overall task of the school.

THE SOCIAL CARE TASK

The greater part of the child's day is spent in the social care environment (rather than the class room). Sound caring practices should be agreed, established and maintained.

The experiences, the relationships and the views of keyworkers towards the child should equate to those of the world outside the school.

Goals should be based upon maintenance and enhancement of personal and social functioning.

Examples of objectives for keyworkers include:

- assisting the child to find solutions in their life;
- encouraging appropriate relationships;
- enabling improvements in self care;
- cultivating appropriate leisure activities;
- enabling independence;
- enabling discharge.

Objectives will not be realised without planning, creating and maintaining the environment in which shared living may take place. This is the primary role of the social care team. Shared living includes:

- developing a meaningful whole, where all – children and staff-take part in decision-making, in determining policy and procedures;
- preparation of children for the world outside, for adulthood;
- a meaningful team approach;
- a healthy climate of debate;
- talking through issues and perspectives.

In many schools a statement of principles on which the life of the school is based is a legal requirement. This should be available to parents, pupils, staff, and where relevant placement authorities. Care principles and procedures should be stated so that pupils are aware of expectations and keyworkers can respond to the child in confidence.

THE SOCIAL CARE CURRICULUM

Teaching and caring practice may be based upon the child's interactions with their physical environment throughout their institutional experience. The goals and techniques of the care worker should parallel those of the teacher and vice versa. Desirable outcomes may be shared and a conscious effort made to deal with the child's functioning in the realities of the present. This avoids (for example) over-emphasising difficulties in one area as the result of 'learning problems'. Competence may be enabled in all areas setting aside the labels and stereotypes brought separately to assessment by both professional cultures.

A curriculum covers all opportunities for learning. Formal occasions, e.g. meals and bedtimes, provide security and consistency and opportunities for social training. Activities and leisure require planning to enable personality adjustment and development of socially mature attitudes and values. Skills development and attitude formation are important dimensions. The role of the keyworker is to make these happen.

Social care aims to meet social, physical, intellectual, cultural, emotional and spiritual needs. Enabling feelings of belonging, safety, security, and identity and achieving full potential are all aspects of these.

Formal experiences and routines in everyday living all contribute to this picture: meal times, serving and clearing; washing, bathing and dressing; visits and visitors; and organised activities (ranging from music/drama to youth clubs, hobbies to discussion groups).

Skills development should be enabled through these

experiences: self care, social skills, speaking and listening skills, agility and dexterity. Classroom experiences should be continued informally in the residential unit: e.g. reading, writing, and drawing. The development of the child's self image (i.e. having positive thoughts and feelings about oneself) gained through activities focusing on daily living in the residential situation may also be achieved by the same positive praise being given in both care and classroom.

Ethical development, social and political awareness and a sense of spirituality will develop over time in residential groups. From this attitudes and values develop e.g. self confidence, self discipline, consideration for others, adaptability, perseverance, concentration, initiative, sensitivity, imagination and tolerance. The informality of group living compliments the formality of the classroom. Building blocks of development should be seen as a whole and discussed jointly by both co-keyworkers.

Leisure opportunities, such as youth clubs, will improve self confidence and help to prepare for roles in society, establishing external standards of behaviour.

Parental participation is required so that continuity is achieved and decision-making is agreed. Routines establishing changes in behaviour or in personal hygiene cannot otherwise succeed, particularly where long holiday periods may be involved. Keyworkers may help parents to overcome feelings of guilt on an admission and to plan for the future.

In building a common personal helping style the links between learning difficulties in the classroom and everyday difficulties of living in care settings will become particularly apparent. For example, focusing upon particular words in reading exercises and finding cooking utensils in a drawer when preparing an evening snack, are both similar problems of perceptual ability. Difficulties in learning to read maps are similar to those involved in helping with the location of clothes to go into the weekly laundry. Social competence is dependent upon language skills; the ability to learn language in the classroom is dependent upon motivation gained from help and reinforcement in the care setting. The development of the child's self image (i.e. having positive thoughts and feelings about oneself) can be achieved by the same positive strokes being given in both care and classroom settings. Co-keyworking involves everyday discussion in assessing and meeting needs, rather than throw away comments tossed at each other in fortnightly staff meetings.

A COMMON PERSPECTIVE

In establishing a coherent whole, staff should aim to work at three levels:

- to define overall philosophies and policies of the school;
- to plan to meet the needs of individual children; and
- to co-ordinate the everyday practice of caring and teaching, where working together on the particular brings benefits on a daily basis.

A common helping style linking learning in the classroom and living in care settings is necessary.

PLANNING FOR INDIVIDUAL NEEDS

The central pivot of these processes is the planning mechanism to meet individual needs. The principles stated in chapter five are now translated into the specific needs of the school setting. Key tenets are thus:

- shared decision-making and agreement between the child's family, care worker and teacher;
- agreement on each worker's primary roles and duties relative to individual issues; duties should complement, and facilitate both the care and teaching task;
- the keyworkers and the school work in close cooperation with the network of all those involved in the service user's welfare (e.g. individuals other professionals and institutions in the locality or community);
- clear benefits to the child;
- purposeful intervention on the child's behalf;

- clear statements of achievable long term goals and short term objectives for the meeting of both educational and social development;
- clear statements of the methods required and persons involved in achieving these objectives;
- clear statements of how methods employed in one setting (classroom or care establishment) will complement and dovetail with those of the other;
- clear statements of how it will be known when goals have been achieved and what are acceptable outcomes;
- details of any constraints which may be imposed and affect the achievement of goals and how these are to be addressed;
- an agreed timescale and mechanism for review.

The process implied here involves more specific elaboration of philosophies of care, and of requirements for the care of individual children than has hitherto been the norm in many schools. Similarly, teachers will need to move beyond processes of statementing under the Education Acts, lesson plans and curricula, to specific individualised planing based in the here and now. In the process of case planning, the potential of sharing ideas, perspectives and achieving tangible outcomes for the child can be realised.

ROLES AND RELATIONSHIPS

The ethos of the residential community is the key to curriculum implementation and the ability to meet individual needs. The school as a whole is more than the mere addition of residence to classroom experiences.

Social care keyworkers are responsible for:

- social training, including accomplishment and competence;
- emotional development helping the process of growing up;
- setting examples and standards of care;
- giving leads in decision-making;

- giving support;
- parental contact to enable secondary parental care.

Mutual recognition between teachers and care staff of roles and the complementary nature of the task will enable essential co-operation. Educational development requires social development.

Roles may overlap yet for co-working should be clearly and accurately defined. Teachers have a responsibility for formal classroom education; social care staff have a responsibility for the non-classroom based development of the child. Both are part of the school team and are involved formally and informally in the joint planning of the child's school experience and development. The social care task and the teaching task, although separate, must dovetail together. The atmosphere in which these separate roles relate together should be one of mutual respect and professional cooperation. This involves sharing perspectives and value bases, so that coherent policy aims and action may be established.

The social care task is carried out by keyworkers acting under considerable emotional pressure. Professional supervision from the head of care based upon clear expectations (so that keyworkers may stand back and examine their work objectively) is required.

Individual care staff or teachers co-keyworking in name only, imposing their own perspectives and interests upon 'their' children is however to be avoided. Paired discussions by care staff and teachers should focus on planning for individual development. The network of such relationships can be used to promote teamwork and lateral communication. Individual wings of the school may thus be less isolated and less immediately dependent upon management for the focus of service user decision-making. Heads of education and care may concentrate more upon their primary task of overall monitoring and professional supervision rather than day to day control. Staff can thus begin to achieve common ground.

Mutual support that keyworkers can offer each other in

these processes should not be underestimated. The hallmark of good practice is the fusing of knowledge and the development of joint strategies. Material presented to reviews based upon the observations and professional opinion of *both* professionals enables a more informed debate to take place. Clarity of expectations enables focused social and educational development. Mutual support enables the management of behaviour problems to be achieved more consistently and in a manner that is less stressful for the workers involved.

The potential for conflict between pairs of co-workers will of course always be there. Conflict is worked through as a priority. The possibility of two workers each pulling in different directions with the child caught in the middle is not discounted. Success is dependent upon coherently shared aims and objectives for the enterprise as a whole. Philosophies must be subscribed to by all the staff involved. The potential for children playing one keyworker against the other is apparent where there is an element of social control within the philosophy of the school.

Whilst co-keyworking may help promote teamwork and communication, without an enabling management style it will be ineffective. Success will breed success. Schools already exhibiting poor or ineffective communication and teamwork may find that co-keyworking (with its dependence upon good communication) may breed a downward spiral of ineffectiveness and inefficiency.

Co-keyworking has considerable spin-offs: teachers increase their responsiveness to the physical space of the classroom setting and the social aspects of education, whilst care staff become more aware of the need to reinforce learning competencies in the care setting.

CONCLUSIONS: A STRATEGY FOR DEVELOPMENT

Social Care and Education are overlapping experiences with a common ground. The whole experience of the child in a residential school is the focus of staff teamwork. A shared philosophy and task may be brought about by the creative welding together of different perspectives and professional ideals. Teachers may tend to place an emphasis upon instrumental educational goals, residential staff upon meeting the child's emotional and physical needs.

Keyworker systems in residential special education establish effective interdisciplinary decision-making, in which children's needs are examined as a whole rather than from a particular perspective. They establish effective interlocking of roles and unified approaches to both care and education.

In developing a strategy for holistic approaches to meeting children's needs, schools will need to develop keyworker systems that countenance:

- adequate training, career development and employment conditions for social care staff;
- sound arrangements for interprofessional communication, and the conduct of relationships, focusing particularly on lateral communication;
- joint working of social care staff and teachers at all levels in the organisation;
- the enabling of teamwork;
- the addressing of any issues revolving around professional 'powerbases';
- the definition and planning of the overall task;
- production of joint statements of individual need;
- production of an overall philosophy and approach that merges the perspectives of care and education.

Thirteen

Keyworking in day care services

INTRODUCTION

In day care services, the keyworker is a named member of staff allocated a particular role in relation to specific service user(s). In some cases they may have a particular relationship with a small group of service users (often known as a 'keygroup'). The keyworker may also take on a wider responsibility for planning and liaison with area teams and other professionals in relation to individual service users. A day centre has a continuing responsibility for bridging the services of day care into the home setting.

The keyworker is the person with the greatest day to day contact with the service user. The relationship between them and the user is of prime importance in advocating and meeting needs. They are the formal link between the service user and the wider staff team, on both a day to day and a continuing basis.

The keyworker will be the person who will pick up any immediate concerns of the user and their situation. Taking any appropriate action. They will be responsible for the input of the day centre into the care planning process (on behalf of the service user) and for progressing the implementation of any decisions made.

This chapter presents illustrative aspects of keyworker practice and discusses the keyworker system found in one particular day centre for persons with a learning disability. The aims of the centre were to develop independence and offer a good quality of life through the provision of opportunities in social and personal tasks, the arts, employment, leisure and community integration. The example shows how a keyworker system may apply within day care. It should be stressed however that this is only one example. The ideas presented here may be translated to fit within the practice at other centres. They may provide structures that may be modified where appropriate to fit practice with other service user groups.

THE RESPONSIBILITIES OF KEYWORKERS IN DAY CARE

Keyworkers were nominated for each of the centre's service users. Their formal role within the context of a personalised relationship was to:

- act as co-ordinator;
- act as a collator of information and resources;
- monitor care planning or individual programme plans;
- act as an advocate for those users unable to advocate for themselves.

In the centre, details of the role of the keyworker were defined in a policy document agreed by the staff team. The document formed a basis for general discussion, supervision, and development of the system. The document is reproduced in full on the next page.

Role of keyworkers

1. To work closely (preferably daily) with individual service users and get to know each on a personal basis.
2. To act as a named person to whom the particular service user relates for support and advice.
3. To liaise with, and get to know, the important people in the lives of the service user – families, carers, friends.
4. To develop action plans to meet the identified needs of individual service users.
5. To monitor programmes along with individual service users. To recommend changes when new needs are identified or when circumstances change.
6. To develop and keep up a personal portfolio with individual service users which can be used as a basis for future assessments/programmes.
7. To ensure that those nominated to work with service users on specific goals understand and accept their responsibilities in relation to action plans.
8. To aid service users in relation to the organisation of their individual programme planing (care planning) meeting.
9. To attend reviews, conferences and planning meetings involving the individual service user.
10. To liaise with other professionals and agencies that could be of benefit to individual service users.
11. To monitor the general health and welfare of each service user and take action as required.
12. To provide a comprehensive induction for each new keygroup member.
13. To be responsible and accountable to the service user and the Department ensuring quick and responsive ways of meeting needs.

The role of the keyworker was found to be of increasing importance in the changing face of community care. Keyworkers have increasingly found themselves carrying out activities beyond those generally taking place within the centre. They examine each service user's situation holistically, considering, for example, user's family and community contacts. Keyworkers at the centre now offer detailed input into assessment/ review systems of other agencies (such as housing associations) on behalf of service users. This is only done with the user's permission. The role is therefore wider than merely carrying out activities within the keyworker's own agency.

This is part of a movement away from centre based services. Provision has become more locally based. The aim of the centre is to make services more responsive to individual needs and choices, working alongside other agencies who have helped to provide additional expertise and opportunities.

Within the centre, keyworkers had a major responsibility towards the service users in their own particular small group. They were expected to keep the management of the centre fully informed of any important matters concerning individual users on a 'need to know basis'. The responsibility was placed upon keyworkers to discuss with their supervisor events of importance and areas of concern. In the same way it was the supervisor's responsibility to pass on relevant information to the keyworker and to give them support and assistance in what they were trying to achieve.

PRODUCING 'PORTFOLIOS' FOR CARE PLANNING

A 'personal folder' or 'portfolio' was used in the keyworker system to generate information for individual programme planning. This enabled the keyworker to record the development of an individual service user. It formed the basis of an assessment procedure which planned programmes with (rather than for) an individual user.

Portfolios worked on the basis that everyone feels a need to know where they have come from. They need to be able to state what they value and stand for, and need to plan what they are aiming for in the future. The system was used to help service users define who they felt they were, and to change other peoples' perception of them. Many users of the centre's services needed support to understand their own lives in a way which allowed them a sense of achievement and identity.

Developing a portfolio was found to help service users to maintain a positive image of themselves as well as giving them some involvement in a process which endeavoured to assess needs holistically.

Personal portfolios/folders were kept confidential to the keyworker and the service user. They contained items relevant to a service user's life space, such as diary notes, photos, drawings, craft work, tape and video recordings as well as written material. Among the information covered were:

- Biographical information such as name, address, age, life history, schools, homes, family links, friends, community contacts etc.
- The user's involvement with the centre – what they do and with whom.
- Likes and dislikes, such as films, music, TV/radio, drinks, food, pop/film stars, clothes. Indications how their tastes may have changed over the years.
- Hobbies and leisure pursuits.
- Areas the user is good at, or areas they may have difficulty with.
- Diary information and landmark events.
- Places the user likes to visit and what do they tend do there.
- Statements of needs. How targets from previous action plans been achieved (and what action has been formulated with the service user if they have not been achieved).

ASSESSMENT AND CARE PLANNING: IPPS

Keyworkers had a responsibility to prepare for individual programme plans (IPPs) along with other staff in their particular work areas. Portfolios formed a basis for progressing assessment. Information in the portfolio gave a much wider picture and complemented other formal techniques. Portfolios enabled targets to be established.

Keyworkers and their supervisors were asked to look at a number of important areas in each service user's life and think how they could move forward. Such areas included: work; leisure; education; home; relationships; and social, physical and material aspects.

After discussing each area with other immediate members of the staff team, keyworkers would look at previous targets and set new ones in discussion with service users and their carers. Once aims were listed keyworkers would examine how, by whom, and when they should be met. The resource implications were also examined at this stage. All immediate staff team members would be involved throughout. A clear concentration on service user competence rather than incompetence was promoted within the team.

Once the keyworker had all this information they were able to come to the IPP meeting with a clear idea of what the user needs were so that decisions could be made involving the user at the meeting.

KEYWORKING AND WIDER ASPECTS OF PROVISION

The full range of the centre's services was laid out in the centre's prospectus. Any combination of the many services on offer was admissible by agreement. Enquiries were welcome from individuals and carers, although applications usually followed an initial assessment conducted by local area social work teams.

The range of services included those that focused upon the community, such as: skills units, joint projects, employment, and voluntary work. Education services were available: Open University, numeracy, literacy, computers, independent living skills, basic concepts education, and sex education. Arts services provided creative outlets: drama, dance, visual arts, and music. The Duke of Edinburgh Award Scheme was available, as well as sports activities. Special provision was made for challenging behaviour, special care, visiting services, and communication. The prospectus also outlined the membership and role of the user's committee, and other means for collective and personal involvement.

The role of keyworkers in coordinating programmes and enabling appropriate use of these services was summarised. Staff were said to be guided by the principles of normalisation and the five accomplishments outlined by Obrien (1981):

- sharing ordinary places;
- making choices;
- developing abilities;
- being treated with respect and having a valued social role;
- growing in relationships.

A CODE OF PRACTICE FOR KEYWORKERS

The prospectus reviewed the code of practice governing the conduct of keyworkers at the centre. By law, service users with learning disabilities have the same rights as any other member of the public. The code of practice made clear that staff have no authority to remove these rights. To safeguard this situation it was important that all the staff group agreed what these rights consisted of, and how they as professionals should respond to ensure rights were not violated.

The code of practice made statements that service users have the right to:

Confidentiality	Service users are entitled to privacy. Personal information relating to users was treated in confidence.
Speak for themselves	All service users have the right to speak their mind. When appropriate an advocate would take this role. Any views or complaints were treated

	seriously.
Dignity and respect	Service users should be treated with respect. Staff activities should be carried out in both a civil and adult manner at all times.
Take risks	The centre accepted that being independent involves a degree of risk taking. They were committed to helping users calculate these risks.
Have relationships	Service users have the right to the normal variety of human relationships.
Community integration	Service users have the same right of access to community facilities as any other member of the public.
Have all their needs considered	A holistic approach was advocated covering leisure time, relationships, health, home, education and employment.
Be consulted and to make choices	Service users will be involved in any decision which relates to them.

Each of these rights were further elaborated with clear guidelines for keyworkers and other staff. These are given in the document overleaf (see pp.166-173).

The rights of service users and a code of practice for keyworkers.

1. THE RIGHT TO CONFIDENTIALITY

Code
Service users are entitled to privacy. All personal information relating to users will be treated in confidence.

Guideline
All written information relating to users is confidential. It should be securely stored.

Service users should not be discussed outside the Unit unless at a user related meeting. Any concerns of the keyworker may be expressed in supervision.

Phone calls relating to users should be done in private and you should be sure of who you are speaking to.

Students and temporary workers who may not be aware of this code should be informed of its importance.

2. THE RIGHT TO SPEAK FOR THEMSELVES

Code
All service users have the right to speak their mind. When appropriate an advocate should take this role. Any appropriate views or complaints must be treated seriously.

Guideline
Keyworkers have a duty to listen to and observe users when appropriate and to respond with constructive advice. When appropriate other indicators such as body language will need to be considered.

There is a formal complaints procedure for all service users. In the first instance if a user makes a complaint about any aspect of the centre's service you should advise and support the user in reporting it to management.

Management will be responsible for discussing the

situation with those involved and deciding what action is to be taken.

After any serious important complaint has been reported to management a decision will be made together with the relevant users and staff as to whether it is valid and whether it is appropriate that it be dealt with by:

1. the users committee;
2. management;
3. the Department's Complaints Officer.

Note that the complaints procedure is quite different from the disciplinary and grievance procedures.

3. THE RIGHT TO DIGNITY AND RESPECT

Code

Service users should be treated with respect, dealings should be carried in both a civil and adult manner at all times.

Guideline

1. Staff should follow the simple rule 'treat users as you would like to be treated yourself' if you were in their position.
   Staff should aim to work along side and have an equitable relationship with users. Staff are not service user's line managers.
2. In the event of a staff member observing one of their colleagues dealing with a service user in what they believe to be an undignified, unreasonable or inappropriate way, it will be their duty under this code of practice to implement the following procedure.
   (a) You should enquire in a supportive way as to the reasons for the behaviour and offer assistance as necessary. Whenever possible this should be done in private.
   (b) If after hearing the explanation you still believe your colleague's behaviour was inappropriate you

should remind your colleague of the dignity and respect part of the code of practice.
At this point the service user should be reminded of their right to complain (or do it for them).

(c) If after further discussion/observation you still feel the situation is unsatisfactory you should report the situation to management.

Note: if you believe you have witnessed what you believe could be classed as gross bad practice you must report it to management immediately.
It is important that you only put the above guidelines into practice if you have witnessed something personally, you should not act upon hearsay. If a colleague confides in you about an incident you need to remind them of their duty under the code of practice.

3. On occasion staff may feel that the general stress of the job is becoming too much, and that you are in danger of 'blowing your top', or are feeling particularly exhausted. If you feel you are approaching this situation you can call in management to arrange for you to a 5 minute time out.
4. Activities and teaching materials should be age appropriate whenever possible.

4. THE RIGHT TO TAKE RISKS

Code
The centre accepts that being independent involves a degree of risk taking, we are committed to helping our users calculate these risks.
Guideline
Staff have a duty to aid users in calculating the risks in any given situation.

Most community based programmes offered by the centre will involve some degree of risk for individual service users as well as the community at large. It is important that we identify the form that any possible harmful results will take as our predicting possible dangers is the first step in preventing them.

Harmful results could be:

1. physical harm to the service user;
2. harm to staff;
3. embarrassment or distress to the service user (reinforcing a cycle of failure);
4. distress or misunderstanding by members of the public;
5. damage to property.

Level of Risk

Once possible harmful results have been identified, we then need to look at the likelihood of them occurring.

Judging this can be difficult and can only really be based on:

1. past experience with an individual in a similar setting;
2. a discussion involving staff and service users which remains hypothetical.

If, after these considerations have been taken into account it's decided that the risk is worth taking, then it will probably be best to 'test out' the situation under carefully controlled and monitored conditions.

It is vitally important not to deny a service user access to an experience purely on hypothetical grounds. However, any discussion should fully explore the seriousness of any possible consequences.

Risk taking policy: summary

- Be prepared to take risks where these involve a service user's personal choice, lead to greater independence, or improve quality of life.
- Any decisions should be well thought out.
- Identify, type and estimate degree of risk.
- Take small steps towards goal.
- Consider less risky alternatives.
- Consider the importance of a goal which involves risk.

- Balance the advantages of the action involving the risk against the disadvantages or taking no action.
- Ensure the service user is aware of the risk and is part of the decision-making process. Consider service user's ability to share personal responsibility for any decision.
- If in doubt 'consult upwards'.
- When major changes are concerned organise team discussion with a team responsibility and written records and plans.

5. THE RIGHT TO HAVE RELATIONSHIPS

Code
Service users have the right to a variety of human relationships.

Guideline
Keyworkers have a duty to advise and offer guidance as to appropriate behaviour that is within the norms of society.

Keyworkers may be requested by service users to have a counselling role. Each individual situation will be different and a strategy for dealing with it must be discussed between the service user and keyworker, and between the keyworker and management. Decisions here should be recorded.

The centre's sex education course is appropriate for a wide range of users. The course concerns relationships with other people as well as increasing the user's personal understanding of sexual development and self awareness. Keyworkers are responsible for making sure that the course is available to service users.

6. THE RIGHT TO COMMUNITY INTEGRATION

Code
Service users have the same rights of access to public facilities as any other member of the public.

Guideline
Keyworkers have a duty to support and encourage service users to take up their right to use normal community facilities. The risk taking policy should be used in deciding the approach to any given situation.

7. THE RIGHT TO HAVE ALL THEIR NEEDS DEFINED

Code
Service users have the right to have all their needs assessed and strategies developed to define and meet these. A holistic approach should be taken which covers the areas of leisure time, relationships, health, home, spiritual needs, physical needs, education and employment (as appropriate).

Guideline
1. Keyworkers have a duty to consider along with users all their individual needs relating to leisure time, relationships, health, home, employment (if appropriate) and education.
   The keyworker system is designed to enable staff to provide an ongoing assessment of need based upon a consistent and long term relationship.
2. Staff must treat all users equally in relation to all aspects of the centre's service. Showing favouritism should be avoided. The aim should be to have an equitable relationship with users.
3. Staff must make the provision of service to users their main priority between the hours of 9.00 and 3.30. During this period they should be aiming to offer quality time to their users.
4. There are some legitimate reasons for being away from your designated activity or key group:
   at a meeting, eg, subgroup, IPP, with managers, etc.;
   visit to WC;
   called to telephone;
   to see to the direct needs of a user.

   You are responsible for/to your group.

If for any reason you need to leave your group unattended for less than 5 minutes you should pass the responsibility on to your nearest colleague. If you need to leave the group for more than 5 minutes you should inform the office and pass responsibility on to them.

This is a general guideline and staff must judge the level of cover a particular group needs. In some cases to leave a group for more than 1 minute would be too long while others could be left to undertake a constructive activity for much longer periods.

5. It is important that you are in place to start your group session within 10 minutes of your start time, eg, 9.30 am, 10.20 am or 1.10 pm. During this period you should make every effort to assemble your group.
6. At the end of the day your group responsibility extends to the moment you pass on responsibility to the transport escort. You must judge the degree of attention you give to this handover as it will vary considerably from user to user. If in doubt consult management.

8. RIGHTS TO BE CONSULTED AND TO MAKE CHOICES

Code

Service users have the right to make choices within the constraints of the stated aims of the Centre. They have the right to be involved in any decision which relates to them.

Guideline

Staff have a duty to provide choices for users within the stated aims of the centre, namely to offer opportunities for independence and advancement through both Centre and community based programmes in the fields of education, the arts, leisure, employment and special needs.

Problems can arise when it becomes necessary to strike a balance between the perceived needs of a user as opposed to their own choice.

The experiences that a user should be offered at the centre should be decided by the user, keyworker, and other staff using range of criteria – the age/lifestyle of the user, previous assessments, users wishes, staff perception/ assessment of users potential, need for experiences on which to base choices.

Users must be consulted throughout this process and offered choices whenever possible. In cases when conflict between choice and need arises management should be involved.

Challenging Behaviour

There will be occasions when staff will feel that a service user's behaviour warrants closer examination. The rights of the service user must be safeguarded in these cases.

Any action as a result of challenging behaviour which goes beyond an immediate 'on the spot' action must be routed through management who will decide in consultation with those involved (including the service user) what the most appropriate response should be, or whether a decision should be facilitated in another forum.

Staff do not have the authority to withdraw any part of the established service without going through the above procedure.

THE KEYWORKER SYSTEM IN ACTION

At this particular day centre, the keyworker was responsible for co-ordinating all aspects of particular service users' programmes and family contact. Evaluation within the system tended to home in on any problems within the user's programme. At an individual level this was based on formal recording and the IPP system. Ongoing every day supervision enabled this to be meaningful. Keyworkers were aware of their responsibilities and would tell their supervisor what was needed and what they need to know. Quality was the benchmark provision.

The keyworker at the centre had a group and would occasionally co-keywork with others. These groups were not necessarily cohesive units. The keyworker was a group leader for their users, but also acted as a link between various other specialised activity groups as was detailed in the prospectus. These structures may be contrasted with other day centres where a keyworker's primary role may be that of facilitator rather than leader of the group.

Supervisors would meet together to talk through general issues and discuss how the system was maintained across the setting. Supervision was not hierarchically based but considered the extent of responsibility and how this linked into wider aspects of role. Every task carried out by a keyworker had its evaluative element. Supervision would lead through issues governed by the worker rather than by the manager. The worker's responsibility was to bring changes in their responsibility and action to managers.

Individual personal programmes at the centre gave a holistic approach in which the keyworker worked with the service user. Keyworkers defined with the user what their wants and needs were according to the user's perceptions. The keyworker would do all and everything for the service user's IPP except chair the meeting.

Thus keyworkers prepared the documents necessary for an IPP beforehand. They projected service user needs and aspirations in order for the meeting to convert these into action. Information collected from the assessment portfolio was reproduced in the form of a report which was used in the meeting. The report concluded with a series of recommendations which if agreed in the meeting eventually formed a 'contract' between the service user, carers and the staff involved. This applied for the following six months (or a lesser period if appropriate and so stated). Service users were encouraged by their keyworkers to present their own report or comments, either written (or verbally) at the meeting.

Keyworkers supported each other in their groups through team roles and activities. The sub-groups in the system were user focused in relation to activities. They met fairly frequently. In addition keyworkers would meet together as groups in order to discuss individual service users, sometimes as often as once a week. The agenda here focused upon the IPP. It examined what the programme could be, reviewed progress, looked at techniques and looked at special needs programming. The keyworker themselves had a clear role here in talking through issues with colleagues.

In general, keyworkers felt that the system was very necessary in order to break down the initiatives of the centre into a more manageable form. In a keyworker group, problems appeared much more personal. Family involvement was facilitated by keyworkers only having eight service users to work with. Keyworkers got very much involved in discussions between parents or carers, outside agencies, the service user and the centre.

Keyworkers felt that their task was to get to know the service user really well, so as to be there when they were needed. The task was to listen to what the service user said. What suited one user did not, of course, suit another. A keyworker needed to pick up on things. It was felt it was good for the user to have someone particular to know so, as to make sense of the IPP system and to network with contacts (for example, work placements and physiotherapists).

Keyworkers were the staff who were particularly aware of the service user's needs. The keyworker kept to the goals of the IPP, but looked very much at the potential of the service user and their independence. This would only works if keyworkers knew users personally and how to work with them. If a service user was undergoing stress and 'having a bad time' the keyworker would have very close contact with them. Their role in some situations would be to discuss things with other parties such as doctors and to monitor the situation informing other staff and being generally supportive to the user.

The centre ran a series of training sessions for keyworkers and other staff. Training for new keyworkers started with induction and then went through an extensive programme over a period of time. This used work based assessment based upon vocational standards. The training in focusing upon the role and responsibilities of keyworkers was directly relevant to their duties. Training and development of keyworkers linked with support in supervision. Specific wider issues for keyworkers were included in the training. These covered the quality of relationships, power, individuality versus the group. identity, quantity and quality of interactions, honesty and the limits of confidentiality. The need on occasions to go beyond the keyworker system, eg. in an emergency, was discussed with all staff. It would, for example be inappropriate to wait until a keyworker was available if a service user had an epileptic seizure.

SUMMARY AND CONCLUSIONS

The keyworker may be seen as the link between the service user and the wider staff group. A keyworker has special rapport with the service user, looking after their welfare. In taking on the wider responsibilities of planning and liaison, keyworkers enable the services in day care to extend into the home and community. They pick up any immediate concerns of the user and their situation. taking appropriate action. Their formal roles consist of co-ordinator, collator of information and resources, monitoring care plans and acting as advocate. These roles centre upon the special relationship between keyworker and service user. Central to this relationship are the joint understanding of needs and how goals may be defined to meet these needs. Such issues are formulated and progressed within the relationship. It is relationships that are the vital currency of keyworking in day care.

Fourteen

Keyworking in domiciliary care

INTRODUCTION: THE NATURE OF THE SERVICE

The development of patterns of keyworking in the domiciliary or 'home care' service cannot be separated from the legacy of its history. Domiciliary care has tended to develop in an ad hoc manner over the last forty to fifty years. The boom time was in the 1970s when many local authorities poured resources into their domiciliary services. The priority was always hands on care, This generally involved some domestic assistance. The supervisory/managerial responsibilities were considered at that time not to be a significant factor. Services therefore developed piecemeal around existing individual managers, rather then there being an appraisal of overall requirements.

The consequent legacy of the period was an average manager workload of around 350 service users involving some 50/60 (usually part time) staff. It was not uncommon at this time to hear of instances of workloads of 800 service users and 140 staff. Clearly where keyworker schemes were said to exist, the supervisory relationship and consequently the service user/keyworker relationship in the context of decision-making and planning had a different shape and feel to that of the other settings that are discussed in this volume.

In the 1980s criticism highlighting the many inherent weaknesses within this formula of service delivery resulted in many authorities improving management structures. This often involved reduced workloads and/or introducing an additional tier of staff. The overall impression was still of a service under managerial/supervisory pressure. The manager's role, loosely speaking, particularly focused upon service assessment/reassessment. The home care assistant focused upon creating relationships and providing a service in the context of the requirements of that assessment

More recently, cut backs in government grant has forced local authorities to re-prioritise services. Many authorities thus reduced the services available to people who were more able. Services were targeted to meet the needs of very dependent people. Part of this strategy was to enhance choice e.g. by giving alternatives to residential care. From this, many specialist services developed such as, home from hospital, and mentally infirm schemes. These schemes are often the bedrock of sound practice. Contracting out services in recent years has in turn brought differing patterns of management and of supervision.

Nationally within the wide variety of types and standards in domiciliary care services, current concerns are the lack of nationally agreed minimum standards and the absence of any requirement for registration and inspection.

This backdrop of variable standards, differing patterns of services, and large spans of managerial control, poses particular issues for the use of the formula of keyworking that is contained in this book.

ISSUES CONCERNING DOMICILIARY KEYWORKER SYSTEMS

It may be said that realistically it is only those service users with high or very high dependency levels that need the structures of keyworking or would benefit from them.

A very high dependency may be said to exist where there

is an inability to remain or return to living in the community without a very high level of appropriate support. Similarly high dependency applies where there is a reliance on others for the maintenance of critical personal needs in order to remain living in the community, or where there is a need to provide a high level of appropriate services to relieve/support the immediate situation.

In both these situations there may be a continuing monitoring role for the home care assistant in the context of the overall assessment plan set by the manager. The planning function and its co-ordination can be carried out by the manager in the context of the intimate personal relationship of the service user and the home care assistant. Manager and assistant can be in constant dialogue in order to maintain the situation and respond to any changing nuances within the context of personal care.

These priority levels of high dependency may be contrasted with low dependency levels, where there is a need for limited/short-term intervention focused upon maintaining minimum hygiene standards or generally improving the quality of life for the individual. Here there may be an increased inability to cope with some of the tasks of everyday life, a temporary absence of a family carer or some other temporary interruption in the service user's quality of life.

Even in situations where, without appropriate levels of support for critical personal needs, there is a danger of deterioration into high dependency, provision generally revolves around occasional assessment and re-assessment. This is rather than the continual dialogue of systems maintenance, and monitoring of provision. These activities on behalf of service users with high dependency levels could be said to need a closer supervision of the home care worker. Similarly care planning structures may utilise aspects of the intense nature of the care assistant/service user relationship.

A high dependency may be triggered by a number of factors:

- hospital or residential care discharge, or the breakdown of highly complex care arrangements leading to an

inability to cope with the tasks of everyday life;
- carer loss or withdrawal, or the carer identifying an unacceptable degree of stress/distress;
- serious mental/physical dysfunction or deterioration, e.g., severe continence problems;
- recent loss of partner, carer, home or a significant change of environment which seriously affects the ability to cope;
- suffering from the effects of living alone/living with relatives or from a dangerous/unsafe physical environment;
- self abuse or abuse from or to others.

Often the service user will be unable to get up or go to bed without assistance or supervision. They may be unable to wash, dress, or bathe themselves without assistance or supervision. Difficulties or inabilities in areas such as, preparing food or feeding themselves without assistance, help with walking, or in performing daily living tasks may have to be tackled in the care plan. The service user may suffer from a psychiatric condition, or serious learning difficulties, or display multiple challenging behaviour. They may have a severe sensory impairment. They may be doubly incontinent

Increasing levels of stress or distress to the carer may necessitate urgent need for support. There may be problems or potential problems in living alone or living with relatives or in a potentially unsafe physical environment.

Generally, only those people who are identified as being of high dependency qualify for services at the weekend. Domestic support may be deemed a low priority and because of the need to maintain levels of individualised care. Many authorities at present keep domestic support under continual review and say it may be reduced or withdrawn at any time. Not all domiciliary care service users would thus need or would choose to have a keyworker.

Services users who have a high dependency level often have the support of their own relative to care (e.g., spouse, partner, daughter, son etc.) and again may not need or choose to have a keyworker.

Formalised keyworker structures are often dependent on effective and meaningful supervision. A large number of Home Care structures do not allow for individual supervision for domiciliary care workers. There is often an assumption by policy makers that because people live in their own homes that they can manage their own lives. However, the numbers if vulnerable individuals living in their own homes are increasing rapidly. There is every sign that this will continue particularly with mentally infirm older people. Trends also indicate that personal carers who are also partners will also become more vulnerable.

Organisational structures which can demonstrate realistic spans of control are able to incorporate keyworking systems for high priority situations. 'Specialist' domiciliary services located in smaller teams with realistic workloads are often thus more able to demonstrate keyworker systems of the calibre advocated in this volume.

The wealth of local information and knowledge that indigenous domiciliary care workers that are recruited to work in the area they live may be utilised to considerable advantage in keyworker systems so that particular needs may be met.

Home care assistants and home helps vary considerably in competence and ability. Any new keyworker system in domiciliary care needs to be targeted to the more competent members of staff. It follows therefore that matching in terms of capability and role is a central issue here. For similar reasons the training of home care assistants is important in maintaining and developing standards. Home care managers who take on a training role in addition to assessment and supervision of staff need particular skills and should be mindful of other priorities within their role. The use of specialist trainers to support home care keyworker systems is therefore advocated.

THE NATURE OF KEYWORKING IN DOMICILIARY CARE

In domiciliary care the keyworker is a named person responsible and particularly accountable for providing individualised social care through decisions relating to the service user's situation. The keyworker may be either the supervisor/manager or may be the home care assistant, depending upon the nature of the system. Where the supervisor is involved, the care assistant is the agent of the supervisor. The roles discussed elsewhere in this book may thus be divided between supervisor and care assistant. Overall, relationships are used to monitor and assess situations in order to make decisions regarding planning and seeing through individualised care.

Keyworking may thus enable a personalised service in domiciliary care. It is also be a means of creating a clear basis for decision-making when more than one person is involved.

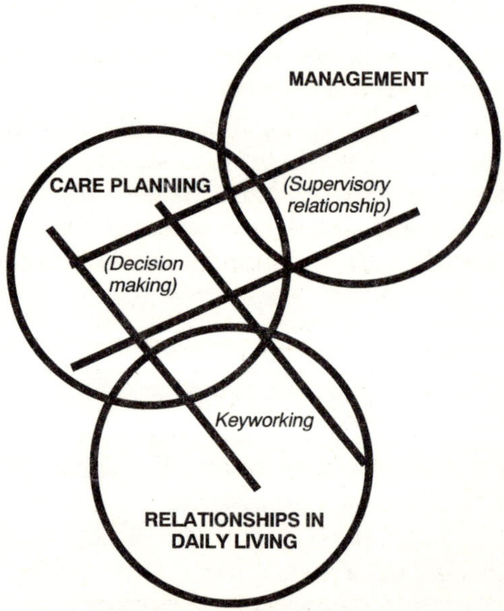

**Keyworking in domiciliary care:
A framework for planning, management and relationships**

In such keyworker systems the three areas of supervision, care planning and relationships in daily living may still be seen to be dynamically related. The activities of the manager and keyworker in linking care planning and relationships are central here. Personalised relationships are used to enable individual needs. This may be illustrated by the previous figure (p.182). This is a variant upon the format previously presented in chapter three.

A KEYWORKER SYSTEM IN MAINSTREAM HOME CARE

Taking one work setting as an example, following the 1990 NHS and Community Care Act, systems involving individual caseload management and designated senior care workers nominated as keyworkers working through home care assistants were implemented. These were formulated alongside individual supervision. Staff were given the responsibility to supply the care needs of their service users each day within parameters defined by the senior care assistant acting as the supervisory keyworker. The new system proved a good motivating factor for home care assistants and provided a structured means to meet needs. Subsequently, for service users who received a high level of individual care, home care assistants were themselves designated as keyworkers.

The role of the keyworker was clearly laid down:

- to ensure that the level of care was maintained;
- to liaise with their supervisor and other home care assistants keeping them aware of the service user's situation;
- to enable the service user to attend Day Centre/Hospital appointments;
- to attend review meetings and discussions;
- to liaise as appropriate with other agencies involved with the service user;
- to ensure care plans, and medication charts were kept up to date.

There were clear aims and objectives formulated around the keyworker's role. This assisted definition of the task and provided a framework for supervision. The aims here were:

- to enable the service to work within the framework of planned care but with the flexibility to respond to changing needs;
- to ensure client participation and involvement;
- to enhance team spirit and strengthen a sense of belonging;
- to increase and maintain communication between home care assistants;
- to improve decision-making;
- to aid motivation and staff development;
- to aid continuity of care to service users.

In order to achieve these aims and provide practice guidelines clarifying and making clear the home care assistant's role a number of policies were agreed for operational practice:

1. Supervision of home care assistants will discuss in detail the aims and objectives of intervention, define what keyworking will involve and the tasks to be carried out. It will set out formally the degree of individual accountability and the limit of decision-making.
2. In each situation, there will be an agreed clear definition of the keyworker's responsibility.
3. All other home care assistants within the particular home care team will need to know who is the designated keyworker.
4. Home care assistants will be advised of the allocated hours per week for each service user. Authorisation must be sought by the supervisor before any permanent or longer term increase in care hours can be made to respond to extra need. However, home care assistants are able to respond to an immediate crisis of short term duration, but must inform their supervisor as organiser as soon as is practical.
5. Group supervision meetings will be held in which each keyworker will take the lead in reporting back on their service users.

Three examples of ways keyworking was used to achieve maximum independence are given below so that the nature of the system may be considered.

Mrs. Smith

Mrs. Smith was 84 years old, living alone in a three bedroomed terraced house. She suffered from chronic arthritis and had gradually deteriorated over many years to the point where she was almost bedfast. She was confined to the front living room where she had a single bed and a commode. There was a door entry system fitted to the property and Mrs. Smith could operate this from her bedside. Although Mrs. Smith was extremely physically disabled she was mentally alert and capable of managing her own affairs.

Mrs. Smith had two sons who were both in their mid-50s. One lived approximately 30 miles away, he was a Licensee and had minimal contact with his mother. The other son lived locally and was known to be an alcoholic. Mrs. Smith had several cousins who visited occasionally.

Mrs. Smith had been receiving the Home Care Service three times daily to provide personal care needs, shopping, laundry, and housework. Mrs. Smith received full attendance allowance, but had to heat her room 24 hours a day. Her fuel bills were excessive.

At present Mrs. Smith was in hospital recovering from a fractured femur. She was very dependent, but refused to consider any form of residential care. She needed two people to arrange movement from her bed and chair.

It was agreed that five visits a day were required to ensure Mrs. Smith's safety and to meet all of her needs.

One of the Home Care Assistants was designated as keyworker. They coordinated the situation over each 24 hour period. As a result of this service Mrs. Smith's choices were fulfilled. She was in full control of her life. Resources were targeted to the greatest need and inappropriate admission to residential care avoided. It was recognised that there would be crisis if there was a breakdown in service. The keyworker monitored the situation closely, and was given support from their supervisor in order to sustain their input.

Mr. Jones

Mr. Jones was 28 years of age and was mentally and physically disabled. His physical disabilities meant that he had no use in his legs and limited use of his arms. He was confined to a wheelchair and needed assistance getting in and out of it. He had been a hospital patient all his life and had had no education. He had a severe speech impediment.

A hospital physiotherapist felt that John had more potential than he was able to achieve in a hospital setting. She arranged for him to be transferred to a hostel for people with learning disabilities. John stayed at the hostel for three years. His progress there was dramatic. He expressed a wish to live on his own. It was arranged that he should move into an adapted bungalow in a small sheltered housing scheme.

His care package was extensive. He attended a Day Centre on five days a week. He also received three visits on weekdays and on Saturday and Sunday an additional visit from two Home Care Assistants at lunch time was planned plus additional time to take John out shopping. A Home Care Assistant was designated as the keyworker as she was the main worker in the situation.

Through her taking this role she was able to consider Mr. Jones' choices in life. Resources were targeted to avoid an inappropriate admission to residential care. The keyworker monitored the situation closely, recognising any difficulties in the early stages and taking action to inform other workers in order to deal with the issues.

Mr. Wood

Mr. Wood was 48 years old and, as a result of an accident at work, had become confined to a wheelchair.

When he first became disabled he lived at home with his mother. She cared for him totally. When she died Mr. Wood went to live with his sister and her husband.

They were very kind to him, but he became very depressed.

It was arranged that he should attend a Day Centre and it was there that he expressed a wish to try and live on his own. The local authority was fortunate in having a half way house for young disabled people to test out their ability to live alone.

Mr. Wood moved in for a trial period and a Home Care Assistant was designated his Keyworker.

He was able to manage most of his own personal care and only needed supervision and minimal assistance when showering and dressing. The major task of the Home Care Assistant was to monitor and assess his ability to manage independently and to report to the Social Worker. The Home Care Assistant was able to say that he would be able to manage on his own. She was then able to assist him to move to his own home.

The strengths of this approach were:

- consistency in assessment;
- reliable feedback and monitoring;
- opportunity to build up a strong relationship between the service user and carer;
- choice fulfilled;
- Mr. Wood controlled his own life.

A SPECIALIST KEYWORKER SYSTEM: THE HOMEMAKER

This system is given by way of contrast to show practices found in a specialist system. The Homemaker system was aimed at rehabilitation in the community for all groups. It focused upon achieving maximum independence for the individual or family.

The Homemaker carried a limited workload and provided a very intensive service. They Homemaker would take on a keyworker role, liaising closely with social workers, providing them with regular feedback on progress.

Clear aims were defined for each of the Homemaker's interventions. A detailed care plan identified the objectives for the Homemaker to achieve. These objectives were agreed with the service user or their family. The Homemaker was supervised by an organiser. Objectives were reviewed and amended during supervision. The focus here was on the role of the Homemaker. When all objectives were complete or maximum independence achieved, a decision whether or not to withdraw the service was considered between the Homemaker and the organiser in supervision sessions.

Later, the Homemaker service concentrated on children and families, and people under 65 with a learning disability or who were in mental distress. The service was particularly successful in supporting young people (who had been living in the care of the local authority) through the transition to independent living.

Realistic work loads and a manageable span of control were the foundations of this service. A commitment by management to maintaining these basic requirements enabled the service to develop, utilising keyworking as the main mode of delivery.

THE COST EFFECTIVENESS OF KEYWORKING IN DOMICILIARY CARE

It can be seen that the main additional costs of keyworker systems in domiciliary care involve:

- more lead in/planning time prior to intervention;
- more time for recording;
- time for supervision;
- identified training needs;
- more attention to planning cover involving greater numbers of staff involved.

Keyworker systems can be particularly cost effective as:

- intervention is focused on the task;
- the service can react to changing needs;
- improved staff morale can reduce absence;
- training relates to job;
- the keyworker 'owns' the work and strives to achieve objectives;
- keyworkers can sustain carers (providing a listening ear).

Keyworker systems can prevent inappropriate admissions to residential care allowing very dependent people to exercise choice and remain in their own homes. Domiciliary workers have more contact with service users in their own homes than any other professional and can provide accurate and reliable feedback of each individual's circumstances and needs.

A FOCUS ON QUALITY

Keyworker systems can be used to provide a quality service in domiciliary care as:

- intervention is focused;
- clear aims/objectives may be detailed in care plans;
- opportunities may be created to change or introduce new objectives in the light of experience;
- opportunities exist for supervisors to assess the value of intervention and abilities of staff;
- opportunities are created for the supervisee to feel valued through supervision improving morale;
- training needs are identified through supervision and may be specifically related to practice improving competence;
- they reduce the possibility of changing staff without agreement;
- they enable the supervisor to identify strengths and weaknesses of supervisees and make best use of these when allocating new work;
- opportunities are created to judge the effectiveness of the service;
- accurate feedback can provide opportunities to give the correct level of care based on experience and knowledge;
- the relationship between the keyworker and service user can enable open and honest discussion;
- a trusting relationship between keyworker and service user may be developed;
- job satisfaction may assist keyworkers in their personal development.

CONCLUSIONS

The foundations of keyworking in domiciliary care involves defined roles, good communication, teamwork, planning, support, clear areas of responsibility and clear philosophies of care. Keyworking practice is monitored via individual supervision, group meetings and visits to service users. Developments in keyworking are taking the home care service forward, bringing a new sense of focus and beneficial ways of working. A cohesive, and integrated approach may be strived for, increasing efficiency and effectiveness.

Fifteen

Keyworking in residential child care

INTRODUCTION

The examples that follow illustrate the diversity of keyworking in child care. A number of instances of keyworking are given, all are different. They all have a common framework, operating the basis of keyworking that is the theme of this book. The common format of the book is translated into different varieties of systems to meet the needs of the different settings involved. Each keyworker system works with the philosophies of the particular units involved.

The common elements of the model discussed in this volume are present in all these examples. These elements enable a focus upon obtaining a clear sense of direction, giving a clear sense of purpose. Keyworker roles are defined by each of the units in relation to individual responsibilities and in relation to the groups involved.

These links between individualisation and the group milieu are particularly important for residential child care. The therapeutic sense of the task is important in creating the keyworker role, and considering this in relation to the work of the staff team and the group care experience as a whole. A key aspect of this is the particular purpose of the unit. From this purpose the particular role of the keyworker is formulated.

A FAMILY SUPPORT UNIT

The first example here, is a family support unit offering short term residential care. The philosophy of the unit is one of goal directed approaches involving change in the family home, as well as with the young person, so that early rehabilitation is possible.

This type of work demands a very flexible approach from the unit's nominated keyworkers. The keyworker, as the main agent in the process of change, will spend many hours in the family home as well as with the young person in the residential unit. Keyworkers are given a clearly agreed role for this involvement within the context of the young person's care plan.

The role of the keyworker is more than that of a 'good parent'. It meets a broad range of needs that have been highlighted as goals in the young person's care plan. The keyworker acts as a role model for changed parenting, providing focused learning involving change for both the young person and their family. These situations are framed with a view to early rehabilitation. The keyworker is also responsible for linking action taken with the young person, and on the young person's behalf, with the needs of other residents, and with the work of the other professionals involved. The role is thus stated in fundamentally different terms from the longer term planning role of the worker from the area team.

Planning the process of rehabilitation

All young people are looked after in the unit within the context of the aims of their own care plan. There is a wide network of partnership involving all those with a legitimate interest in the welfare and development of the young person.

The keyworker has to fulfil areas defined by regular planning meetings. They have clear professional accountability. This is in the context of the residential unit providing a service which addresses particular targeted needs within a wider, clearly defined, targeted, and time-limited strategy.

The start of this process of planning for the young person during their stay in residential care is the establishment of a clear rationale for the use of the residential resource and the role of the keyworker. The residential resource and the skilled services of the nominated keyworker that come with it, are a scarce commodity that have to be used efficiently and effectively. The potential of the young person and their situation have to be examined carefully in relation to how these resources may be used. The process matching keyworker and young person, focuses upon the task in hand and the professional attributes that will be involved.

Roles are customised and are not driven by the old model of conveyor belt care. The potential for change activated by the keyworker as a catalyst acting in a particular role focuses upon the task in hand. Professional caring in these circumstances demands clear thinking and a task centred approach. Choice, freedom and individual support are not lost, rather they are incorporated within a clear goal directed focus upon change, as the overriding purpose of the exercise.

Often the young people who are involved in these processes have previously undergone many difficulties in their lives. Until now family or placement breakdown will have reinforced strongly obtained skills of working in 'negative' or manipulative ways to gain what they wish, or they believe they may wish, to achieve. These games have negative pay-offs. Where this is recognised by the parties concerned, residential care utilising the short term rehabilitative model, agreed to in advance by consumer choice of the young person and their family will be appropriate. The keyworker may reshape the thinking of the parents and the young person, re-engineering the basis of association, agreeing and negotiating time spent together again in freshly considered relationships.

The keyworker will not be involved longer than they need to be. They will not create emotional ties or dependency. The families involved are left together with problems of relationships solved and with new strengths, pursuing joint activities and able to address subsequent problems as a family group. Re-referral is a later option should further short term intervention be necessary again in the future.

The role of the keyworker in the context of the team

Within these processes the role of the keyworker must be clear and well defined. Keyworking is more than a supportive role, it also concerns professional advocacy. The traditional role of the keyworker in a 'buddy relationship' has been moved aside. The role involves more than informally representing the young person's feelings within the staff group and other internal forums, the keyworker is now seen as a professional and accountable agent. Advocate and friend are not interchangeable. The role of keyworker is in this project one of professional accountability for service delivery through the care plan.

The keyworker is accountable for action within this role. Partnership is the keynote. Hearing the voice of the young person involves a wider team than just the keyworker. Bed times and quieter reflective moments within the residential unit offer time for talking issues through. A skilled and quick thinking keyworker will both befriend and act as advocate as well as doing the much wider actions demanded by their role. The keyworker must make sure that thy do not isolate the young person from the wider social experience available within the residential unit. The caring function is also a team function if the full potential of residential care as a powerful form of intervention is to be utilised.

Management of the keyworker system

Supervision and training of keyworkers was felt to be vital so that keyworkers can carry out their role to their best ability. As defined here the role is highly skilled. It required a great deal of sensitivity and co-ordinative ability. Supervision tended to be task related based on issues that were happening in the here and now of practice, setting long and short term goals with the keyworker. Managers needed to ensure that keyworkers know exactly what they are doing, why they are doing it, and how they are doing it. The selection of a suitable keyworker and the service they offer is a managerial issue. There is agreed to be no place for 'vacancy takes the next referral' in the process of matching keyworker to young people in this unit.

Management, and support of keyworkers and the maintenance of the keyworker system was a high priority. Management of the system was an important plank in creating the platform for the relationships upon which keyworking was to depend. Managers needed to ensure clear and effective user centred recording. Keyworkers needed to be clear about their role in partnership with the wider network of care. Managers needed to constantly review and question the value base of the service.

A consumer's view of keyworking

Young people who had used the services of the unit were asked for their views of their keyworkers:

> *Keyworkers are supposed to listen.*
>
> *My keyworker was excellent, he got me to trust in men again.*
>
> *If I asked him to come to a meeting he would come.*
>
> *They are supposed to help you with your family situation.*
>
> *She never used to talk to me, I didn't really get on with her.*
>
> *I've got two keyworkers and they are always there to listen, you can have a laugh when you're having serious talks.*
>
> *They used to spend loads of time with me.*

I got bunged on her, she felt that everything I wanted she had to do.

I was sitting upstairs one day and she came up to take to me. She gave me chewing gum and started talking about my problems and she said that because she had given me something I had to give her something you know, like my problems and I didn't want to tell her, because I didn't trust her.

I still see my keyworker they keep in contact with me, he phoned me I didn't phone him, it felt good.

KEYWORKING AT 'THE HOUSE'

Keyworking at 'the house' may be contrasted with that of the family support unit. 'The House' was a temporary resource unit in a school setting offering close support in a family style setting. The five male residents each with individual needs formed a group context with considerable tensions. These were managed by a new staff team of four all of whom had considerable experience of the work. Enthusiasm and the need for close support for individuals in the group context dictated a particular form of keyworker system.

The unit was set up from scratch involving the boys in all decision-making and activities such as furnishing and decorating. This was carried out having regard for individual tasks, and the capabilities and identities of the young persons involved.

The team commitment and the joint ethos placed keyworking in a wider context. The focus and responsibility for individual work was the keyworker's, yet in a small interactive space away from the main establishment, close relationships within the whole group were dictated. This demanded clear and frequent communication between keyworker and colleagues.

The keyworker's role was one of co-ordination and monitoring plans. The group context and the group approach did not demand exclusive relationships. Keyworking gave staff confidence and gave a focus to care planning. Inexperienced members of staff worked closely with their supervisors. Positive relationships were the antidote to any negative behaviour by the young people, the strong team ethos welded individuality and group approaches.

In the enthusiasm for the new project, relationships developed that enabled close supportive supervision. Staff were able to quickly identify patterns of behaviour and pointers to the management of behaviour. Strong relationships were developed between individual young people and their keyworkers, whilst at the same time the small group setting had a firm team context and ethos. The keyworker's task was to give and receive information concerning their particular young person. House staff meetings were important forums involving all staff in the context of a child centred approach. The keyworker / young person relationship was not an exclusive one as all relationships were strong whether or not the staff member was the young person's keyworker.

The keyworker undertook specific tasks. They had the responsibility to update the child's care plan and assess progress. They updated their colleagues in weekly house meetings covering a range of issues:

- education;
- behaviour;
- any serious incidents;
- any legal matters; and
- contact with outside agencies, and social workers.

They focused upon the present and future plans for the child. They were a point of reference within the staff team and for the child. The keyworker would receive and promote feedback from other staff regarding perceptions of progress and any emerging or longstanding patterns of behaviour. They would seek information and give information with the goal of ensuring a consistent approach by the staff team.

Recognising specific behaviour problems exhibited by the children lead keyworkers to frequently undertake liaison with social workers and with the child's family. 'Hands-on' experience gave confidence in interchanges with family members.

Supervision was particularly important to hold the overall agenda together. The focus upon the task and upon progress concerned the education of workers depending upon their experience. New staff members were allocated a co-worker to shadow so that the child centred commitment became the overall motivation.

Examples of keyworking in operation

With one child the keyworker instituted a behaviour programme by identifying specific areas for the young person to work on. These included his language, settling at bedtime, and controlling his anger. These areas were identified by the keyworker concerned through personal observation with assistance from other staff and the young person himself. Supervision provided a reflective sounding board enabling the keyworker to talk through the issues involved. The social worker attended meetings involving decision about the programme. All staff were briefed by the keyworker to guarantee consistency in approach. The keyworker's role as 'change agent' was to ensure that all concerned (including the young person) were aware of the expectations of the programme and that the results and the young person's progress were monitored.

An important task for keyworkers was to enable children to integrate into the day school whilst resident at the house. In one instance the keyworker attended the school with the young person for the first week, to become familiar with the teaching task and help staff to deal with specific behaviour problems, encouraging consistency between school and the house. A diary system was then instituted by the keyworker in which house and school staff made daily entries into the young person's special book. The young person took this between the house and the school so that everyone (including the child himself) was made aware of progress.

In another situation the compilation of a life story book

was instituted by the keyworker. The special relationship between the young person and the keyworker provided a focus for joint explorations of the young person's life. The family tree, the photo album and record of movements in the child care system were important to the young person in making sense of the situation they were now in. The keyworker supported them during their period of residence which was required to conduct an assessment. Preparation for the subsequent move, liaison with staff and resources, arranging support systems and maintaining continuity were primary aspects of this task. Keyworking provided a particular focus for this. The relationship was of central importance. The keyworker liaised regularly with the young person's family. They looked to him for support and the point of contact gave them confidence in the future and the sense of direction that the keyworker's plans gave to the youngster.

A THERAPEUTIC SUPPORT UNIT

The context: a group milieu

Here the creation of a caring and trusting 'milieu' was felt to be the main foundation in creating a context for the young person to mature in an appropriate way. The level of disturbance in their lives that young people in care had experienced was also felt to need more than just the caring milieu if needs were to be met. Radical short and medium term intervention needed to give appropriate boundaries and stability to damaged lives.

There were four areas in the overall philosophy of the unit:

- meeting day to day needs;
- the group context;
- a planned programme;
- and co-ordinating and managing planned care.

These all focused on the young person achieving their maximum potential. The keyworker relationship with the young person was vital to achieving in all these areas.

The keyworker's role

The keyworker's role concerned enabling, co-ordination and liaison. They were not there to do everything, rather they made sure that needs were met and that tasks were achieved and that agency functions were fulfilled.

The needs of young people were seen to focus upon love and security, praise and recognition, responsibility and the need for new experiences. Building upon the personal nature of the intimate trust within the keyworker/ young person relationship gave a clear platform for work in these areas. The keyworker co-ordinated assessment and ways of meeting these needs.

The group context provided a rolling programme of educative activities as well as relationships in the context of everyday living. Keyworkers were involved in flagging up to the groupworker and other staff issues that were current for their keychild.

The planned programme was proactive consisting of activities such as life story books and reactive problem solving. Activities here included day to day tasks, monitoring health, and family contact. The keyworker's role was one of the primary agent in instituting and managing these.

In co-ordinating, managing and evaluating planned care the keyworker took a lead relative to individual young people they had a responsibility for. This involved reviews, children's panels and meetings. They produced reports and prepared the young person for the events and ensured that all staff members acted upon programmes that were agreed. The keyworker was responsible for ensuring that the person who was most appropriate carried out the tasks involved. A monthly evaluative report was prepared, this focused upon what had been achieved and what was still outstanding.

Evaluation of the introduction of the system indicated that there were clear benefits from the intensive work of the keyworker.

The main benefits of keyworking were said to be planning, co-ordination, and productive relationships. The young people in the unit had experienced multiple emotional, physical and sexual abuse. In many cases they had also experienced a number of caring situations that had broken down. They all had a history of psychiatric involvement, and within the care system a historic need for restraint and containment. Keyworking with its stress on relationships broke down barriers and improved the young people's notion of self control. All planned work was carried out under the consultancy of the child psychiatrist and the focus obtained by co-ordination through the role of the keyworker enabled consistency and clear arrangements for monitoring effect.

The role of the supervisor was to enable keyworkers to make sense of their task. Through regular staff monitoring of the system, the learning experienced was transferred to the whole staff team. The keyworker was accountable through supervision. In sessions they would conjointly examine what was happening and how the needs of the child were being defined and met.

Keyworking was taken on with enthusiasm enabling clear practice and outcomes. A previous tendency to defensiveness was now being put aside. The keyworker and the supervisor shared roles within the culture of the team ethos. In relation to short term tasks the keyworker would carry these out under supervision and within the context of the overall structure and ethos of the unit, Long term tasks were planned by the keyworker with the team in the form of individualised programmes. The keyworker negotiated these programmes with the members of the team and under the consultancy of the child psychiatrist. The team was defined collectively as the primary therapist but the keyworker was the co-ordinator of the context of that therapy.

In integrating programmes with the therapeutic task of the unit, aims and objectives and their attainment were constantly checked out by the keyworker. The plans had a contractual nature within the ethos when the assumptions were agreed within the staff team. The supervisor would facilitate and keep the staff group and keyworker focused upon the task.

An example of a programme to modify behaviour

Taking the example of 'John', aspects of the keyworker role in operation may be examined. A planned programme of reactive work was instituted by the keyworker aiming to help him live within externally imposed boundaries. It was planned to induce changes in behaviour. This was carried out in the context of other work by the keyworker to ensure that needs were met and an overall planned programme was pursued.

On each occasion where standards of behaviour were felt to be unacceptable, John was taken on one side in a separate room and the issues talked through. Examples of occurrences were those involving the invasion of other people's 'personal space' and verbal or physical aggression. The keyworker had to work hard to ensure that all staff on duty were clear about the programme and how these incidents were to be handled.

Early sessions established ground rules, later sessions focused upon acceptable standards and the effect of attitudes and processes that had resulted in 'winding other people up'.

John was consistently resistant to these sessions. They had to be carefully managed. The staff and the keyworker decided the agenda and issued challenges to avoidance techniques. Over a period of time, John's reaction became calmer and more settled and change began to be effected.

John began to make progress to develop sufficient internal controls to prevent himself getting involved in certain situations. He also, however, became more adept at manipulating situations away from staff, so reducing the number of times he was observed exhibiting problematic behaviour. Overall it was felt, after some three months, that John had benefited from the programme devised by the keyworker and the programme was refocused to meet the changed situation.

Proactive work with John also consisted of planned activities and outings co-ordinated by the keyworker and undertaken with other staff. These included relaxation and exercise sessions focused upon ways of calming himself down, visits to leisure centres (swimming pool and gym) giving an opportunity to integrate within a larger group whilst still under staff support, and shopping trips accustoming John to busy places. At other times, John exercised his right to chose not to go out.

John responded positively and enthusiastically to these activity schedules. Behaviour was reported to be of an acceptable standard

In receiving regular staff/keyworker attention within an appropriate framework, John exhibited a decrease in inappropriate demanding of attention. He learnt to make many choices and formed positive relationships with a number of people. He began to show signs of being able to live within societal boundaries. He became less aggressive. The frequency of reactive work in emergencies reduced considerably over this period. A sense of impulse control was engendered. Over the period a sense of greater stability enabled a more productive building of relationships.

The keyworker's role in devising, co-ordinating and monitoring these programmes was central to their effectiveness. The sense of focus for all concerned and placing them in the context of an overall planning strategy to meet wider needs was felt to be essential.

CONCLUSIONS

The apparent diversity of keyworking in child care is unified by utilising a common framework. Each keyworker system works with the different philosophies of the particular units involved.

All the elements involved have a common focus enabling a clear sense of direction within the system. The importance of the keyworker's role relative to care planning and co-ordination of the experience within the group should not be minimised. Individual responsibilities link with the group milieu as an important context for keyworking in all these residential child care settings. The therapeutic sense of the task is important in considering the nature of the keyworker role, and considering this in relation to the work of the staff team and the group care experience as a whole.

Keyworking achieves here the individualisation required for effective relationships, it enables a sense of focus and continuity through planning. It advocates need, it harnesses the skills of the team as a whole relative to the individual young person. Keyworking is the link between individualisation and the group. It is a system that enables the best in child care.

References

Adair J (1973) *Action Centred Leadership*, Gower, Aldershot.

Alkin M (1971) *A Theory of Evaluation*, University of California, Los Angeles.

Allen -Meares P & Lane BA (1987) Grounding Social Work Practice in Theory: Ecosystems, *Social Casework*, October, Family Service America (pp 515-521).

Anderson, D (1982) *Social Work and Mental Handicap*, Macmillan, Basingstoke.

Argyris C & Schon DA (1974) *Theory in Practice, Increasing Professional Effectiveness,* Jossey-Bass, San Francisco.

Atherton JS (1986) *Professional Supervision in Group Care, A Contract-Based Approach*, Tavistock, London.

Atherton JS (1989) *Interpreting Residential Life: Values to Practise,* Tavistock/Routledge, London.

Baldwin (1990) *The Power to Care in Children's Homes*, Avebury, Aldershot.

Bartlett, HM (1970) *The Common Base of Social Work Practice*, National Association of Social Workers, New York.

BASW (1985) *Report on the Management of Child Abuse*, British Association of Social Workers, Birmingham.

Beardshaw V & Towell D (1990) *Assessment and Case Management,* Kings Fund, London.

Beresford P & Croft S (1986) *Whose Welfare- Private Care or Public Services?,* Brighton Polytechnic.

Berry J (1975) *Daily Experience in Residential Life*, RKP, London.

Bertcher H & Garvin C (1969) Staff Development in Social Welfare Agencies, Proceedings of an Institute held at the University of Michigan School of Social Work, May 1968, Ann Arbour, Michigan: Campus Publishers. Quoted in Douglas R & Payne C (1988) *Organising for Learning*, National Institute for Social Work, London.

Bettelheim B (1974) *A Home for the Heart*, Thames and Hudson, London.

Bowlby J (1963) *Child Care and the Growth of Love*, Penguin, Harmondsworth.

Braithwaite R (1988) Creating a Place of Solace, *Community Care*, 27-10, Wallington (pp 22-23).

Brent, London Borough of (1985) *A Child in Trust*, London Borough of Brent.

Bromley G (1977) Interaction Between Field and Residential Social Workers, *British Journal of Social Work*, Vol. 7 No 3 (pp 285-299).

Brown B (1986) Reliability of the Staff Performance Rating Scale, *Orchard Lodge Studies of Deviancy*, Vol. 6, No. 1, Winter, London.

Brown D & Brearley P (1990) Homes in a Warm Climate, *Insight*, 4 July, London (pp 24-27).

Burningham S (1983) Who Makes the Rules?, *Social Work Today*, 25-10, Birmingham (pp 10-11).

Burns T & Stalker GM (1961) *The Management of Innovation*, Tavistock, London.

Butler B & Elliott D (1985) *Teaching and Learning for Practice*, Gower, Aldershot.

Cambridge P (1992) Case Management in Community Services: Organisational Responses, *British Journal of Social Work*, Vol. 22, October, Oxford University Press (pp 495-517).

Caroll SJ & Tosi H (1973) *Management by Objectives - Allocations and Viewpoints,* Macmillan, New York.

CCETSW (1973) *Social Work: Residential Work is Part of Social Work*, Paper 3, Central Council for Education and Training in Social Work, London.

Challis D (1985) in Hatch S (Ed) *Decentralisation and Care in the Community*, Discussion Paper No. 10, Policy Studies Institute, London.

Challis D & Davies B (1986) *Case Management in Community Care*, Gower, Aldershot.

Challis D, Darton R, Johnson L & Stone M (1988) Multi-Skilled Carers in the Community, *Social Work Today*, 4-8, London (pp 13-15).

Challis D, Darton R, Johnson L, Stone M, Traske K & Wall B (1989) *Supporting Frail Elderly at Home*, PSSRU, University of Kent, Canterbury.

Clark CL & Asquith S (1985) *Social Work and Social Philosophy, A Guide for Practice,* Routledge and Kegan Paul, Library of Social Work, London, Clifton.

Clough R (1986) Staffing of Residential Homes in Judge K and Sinclair I (Ed) *Residential Care for Elderly People*, HMSO, London.

Collins T & Bruce T (1984) *Staff Support and Training*, Tavistock, London.

Cooper DM & Ball D (1987) *Social Work and Child Abuse*, Macmillan Education, Basingstoke.

Cotmore R, Sinclair R, Webb A & Wistow G (1985) Five Faces of Care, *Community Care*, 27-6, Wallington (pp 15-18).

Coulshed V (1990) *Management in Social Work*, Macmillan Practical Social Work, Basingstoke.

Dant T & Gearing B (1990) Keyworkers for Elderly People in the Community: Case Management and Care Coordinators, *Journal of Social Policy*, Vol. 19 No 3 July (pp 331-360).

Dant T, Gearing B, Carley M & Johnson M (1989) *Keyworkers for Elderly People in the Community: Case Mangers and Care Coordinators*, Care of Elderly People at Home Project Paper No.6, Open University Department of Health and Social Welfare/ Policy Studies Institute, Milton Keynes.

Darvill G & Smale G (Eds) (1990) *Partners in Empowerment: Networks of Innovation in Social Work. Pictures of Practice*, Vol II, National Institute for Social Work, London.

Davis L (1978) Beyond the Keyworker Concept, *Social Work Today*, 10-1, Birmingham (p 17).

Davis L (1982) *Residential Care: A Community Resource*, Heinemann, London.

Davis L (1985) When the Rules Take Over, *Social Work Today*, 29-7, Birmingham (p 19).

Department of Health (1988) *Protecting Children - A Guide for Social Workers Undertaking a Comprehensive Assessment*, HMSO, London.

DHSS (1976) *Non-Accidental Injury to Children*, Area Review Committees, Circular LASSL<76>2/CMO<76>2, Department of Health and Social Security, London.

DHSS (1979) *Residential Care for the Elderly in London*, Social Work Service, London Region, cited in Lishman J (1982) *Developing Services for the Elderly*, Research Highlights in Social Work No 3, University of Aberdeen, Kogan Page, London.

DOH (1990) *The Care Programme Approach for People with a Mental Illness Referred to the Specialist Psychiatric Services*, Joint Health/Social Services Circular HC(90)23/LASSL(90)11 Department of Health, London.

DOH (1993) *Guidance on Standards for the Residential Care Needs of People with Specific Mental Health Needs*, HMSO, London.

Dominelli L (1988) *Anti-Racist Social Work*, Macmillan, Basingstoke.

Douglas R & Payne C (1980) What Happened to the Keyworker Idea, *Social Work Today*, 21-10, Birmingham (p 16).

Douglas R & Payne C (1987) *Learning about Caring, An Introductory Package for Staff Development in Residential and Day Care Work*, National Institute for Social Work, London.

Douglas R & Payne C (1988) *Organising for Learning*, National Institute for Social Work, London.

Douglas R, Ettridge D, Fearnhead D, Payne C, Pugh D & Sowter D (1988) *Helping People Work Together: A Guide to Participative Working Practices,* National Institute for Social Work, Paper 21, London.

Douglas T (1986) *Group Living*, Tavistock, London.

Department of Health/ Scottish Office (1991) *Care Management and Assessment, Managers' Guide,* HMSO, London.

Dubois D, Mockler B & Mockler G (1984) Foster Parents as Keyworkers/ Work with Natural Parents, *Adoption and Fostering*, No. 3, British Association of Adoption and Fostering Agencies, London (pp 30-33).

Dunham J (1980) The Effects of Communication Difficulties on Social Workers, *Social Work Today*, 29-1, Birmingham (pp 10-12).

Elkan R & Kelly D (1991) *A Window in Homes: Links between Residential Care Homes and the Community,* Social Care Association, Surbiton.

Elliot D (1978) Integrated Methods and Residential work, *Social Work Today*, 14-2, Birmingham (pp 11-14).

Elliot D (1980) Some Current Issues in Residential Work: Implications for the Social Work Task in Walton RG & Elliott D (Eds) *Residential Care: A Reader in Current Theory and Practice,* Pergamon Press, Oxford.

Elliot D (1982) A Second Opinion, *Social Work Today*, 6-4, Birmingham (p 15).

Farrar J & Tierney T (1985) Joint Evaluation by Worker, Supervisor and Client, *FSU Quarterly*, May 1985 (pp 33-37)

Ferlie E, Challis D & Davies B (1989) *Efficiency-Improving Innovations in Social Care of the Elderly*, Gower, Aldershot.

Ferlie I, Pahl J & Quine L (1984) Professional Collaboration in Services for Mentally Handicapped People, *Journal of Social Policy,* Vol. 13 Part 2, Cambridge University Press, Cambridge (pp 188-202).

Fletcher J (1985) Have You Ever Thought of Living in a Home? in in McDerment L & Greengross S (Eds) *Social Care for Elderly People,* An International Perspective, Social Care Association, Surbiton.

Forrest A (1984) *Delegation*, Industrial Society, London.

Fulcher LC & Ainsworth F (1985) *Group Care Practice with Children,* Tavistock, London.

Gardner R (1987) Children's Participation in Care Decisions, *Adoption and Fostering*, Vol. 11 No 2, London (pp 12-14).

Garland DSR (1987) Residential Child Care Workers as Primary Agents of Family Intervention, *Child and Youth Care Quarterly*, Human Science Press (pp 21-34).

Giddens A (1979) *Central Problems in Sociological Theory, Action, Structure and Contradiction in Social Analysis*, Macmillan, London.

Glendinning G (1986) *A Single Door, Social Work with Families of Disabled Children*, Allen and Unwin, London.

Goffman E (1961) *Encounters*, Bobbs-Merrill, Indianapolis.

Goldstein, H (1973) *Social Work Practice a Unitary Approach*, University of South Carolina Press, Colombia.

Gray B & Isaacs B (1979) *Care of the Mentally Infirm*, Tavistock, London.

Hambleton R and Hoggett R (1990) *Beyond Excellence: Quality Local Government in the 1990s,* Working Paper 85, University of Bristol School of Advanced Urban Studies.

Hanvey C (1987) Social Work as She is Spoke, *Community Care,* 30-4, Wallington (pp 16-17).

Harris D (1975) Personal View, Tinker, Tailor, Fieldworker, Residential Worker, *Social Work Today*, 6-2, Birmingham (p 693).

HMSO (1989) *Caring for People, Community Care in the Next Decade and Beyond*, HMSO, London.

Hogan M (1988) Matching a Keyworker to the Needs of the Client, *Social Work Today,* 28-4, London (p 27).

Howe J (1990) The Croxteth Park Project, *Social Care Education,* No 8 Sept/Oct, Social Care Association, Surbiton (pp 21-22).

Hudson J (1981) A Staff to Support Your Value System, *Social Work Today*, 14-7, Birmingham.

Hulley T (1985) Let's Give the Client Responsibility, *Social Work Today*, 6-5, Birmingham (p 17).

Hunter DJ (1988) *Bridging the Gap: Case Management and Advocacy for People with Physical Handicaps*, King Edward's Hospital Fund, London.

Isaac S & Mitchel M (1981) *Handbook in Research and Evaluation*, Sage.

Jack R (1986) The Assessment of the Elderly Mentally Ill, *Action Baseline*, Spring, London (pp 15-18).

Johnson S (1981) Staff Cohesion in Residential Treatment, *Journal of Youth and Adolescence*, Vol. 10 No. 3.

Johnson S (1982) Staff Cohesion in Residential Treatment, *Child Care Quarterly*, Vol. 11, Part 3, Fall (pp 204-210).

Johnston S (1988) The Implementation of a Keyworker System in Mallinson (Ed) *Social Care Practice with Elderly Persons*, Social Care Association, Surbiton.

Jones M (1968) *Beyond the Therapeutic Community, Social Learning and Social Psychiatry,* Yale University Press, New Haven.

Kadushin A (1976) *Supervision in Social Work*, Colombia University Press, New York.

Kelly D (1987) Working towards New Relationships for Residents and Staff, *Social Work Today*, 13-4, Birmingham (p 25).

Kelly D & Beck M (1990) Home Front: The Power of Choice, *Community Care Supplement*, 7 June, Wallington.

Ledger R (1980) Residential Turnover - Should You Remain at Your Post?, *Social Work Today*, 17-6, Birmingham (pp 20-21).

Lee P & Pitters D (1980) Radical Residential Child Care: Trojan Horse or Non-runner? in Brake M & Bailey R (Eds) *Radical Social Work and Practice*, Edward Arnold, London.

Leigh A (1989) When a Manager's Personal Style Inspires Creativity, *Social Work Today,* 21-9, London (pp 20-21).

Lishman J (1982) *Developing Services for the Elderly*, Research Highlights in Social Work No 3, University of Aberdeen, Kogan Page, London.

Mallinson I (1987a) Key Objectives, *Insight*, 20-11, London (pp 20-22).

Mallinson I (1987b) Care Without Conflict, *Insight*, 18-9.

Mallinson I (1989a) The Key to Keyworking, *Social Work Today*, 30-3, London (p 28).

Mallinson I (1989b) The Key to Meeting Each Child's Needs, *Social Work Today*, 14-12, London (pp 16-17).

Mallinson I (1989c) Sustaining the Cornerstones of Practice, *Insight*, 7-6, London (pp 20-21).

Mallinson I (1989d) The Key to Economy Efficiency and Effectiveness, *Insight*, 9-5, London (pp 12-13).

Mallinson I (1993) *Keyworking in Residential Care*, Unpublished PhD thesis, University of Warwick.

Mallinson I & Best E (1987) Sharing Tasks will Mean More Client Choice, *Social Work Today*, 7-12 (pp 12-13).

Mallinson I & Citarella V (1990) Making the Perfect Match, *Community Care*, 26-4, Wallington (pp 27-29).

Menzies EIP (1967) *The Functioning of Social Systems as a Defence Against Anxiety*, Tavistock, London.

Meteyard B (c.1986) *Keyworker Shop*, Local Government Training Board, Luton.

Meyer E (1986) *A Study of Organisational Reform: An Examination of the Impact of Organisational Structure on Staff Attitudes Within a Residential Setting for Mentally Retarded Persons*, Brandeis PhD, February 1986, abstract in *Social Work Research and Abstracts*, Vol. 22, National Association of Social Workers, New York (p 42).

Mitchell TR (1983) *People in Organisations, An Introduction to Organisational Behaviour*, McGraw Hill, Aukland.

Moore J (1985) *The ABC of Child Abuse Work*, Gower, Aldershot.

Morrison T (1986) Teamwork: Beyond The Sum of Its Individuals, *Community Care*, 4-9, Wallington (pp 26-28).

NISW (1982) *Social Workers: Their Roles and Tasks* (The Barclay Report), National Institute of Social Work, London.

NISW (1988) *Residential Care, A Positive Choice*, Report of the Independent Review of Residential Care, Chaired by Gillian Wagner, National Institute of Social Work, London.

O'Brien J (1981) *The Principle of Normalisation: A Foundation for Effective Services*, Values into Action, London

Pettes DE (1979) *Staff and Student Supervision,* National Institute for Social Work, London.

Phillips J (1986) Tools of Care: Planning and Managing the Care Environment, *Social Work Education*, Vol. 5 Pt 2, Summer (pp 16-19).

Pincus A & Minahan A (1973) *Social Work Practice: Model and Method,* Peacock, Itaska.

Plank M (1982) *Teams for Mentally Handicapped People*, Enquiry Paper 10, The Campaign for Mentally Handicapped People, London.

Pope P (1982) A New Approach, *Community Care*, 2-12, Wallington (pp 18-19).

Quine L & Pahl J (1989) *Stress and Coping in Families Caring for a Child with Severe Mental Handicap: A Longitudinal Study*, University of Kent Canterbury.

Ragg HM (1977) *People Not Cases- A Philosophical Approach to Social Work*, Routledge and Kegan Paul, London.

Raven BH & Rubin JZ (1976) *Social Psychology: People in Groups*, Wiley, New York.

RCA/BASW (1976) How Can Residential and Field Social Workers Co-operate?, *Social Work Today*, 2-9, Birmingham (pp 346-348).

RCA (1978) *Heads and Hearts*, Residential Care Association, London.

RCA (1983) The Keyworker, A Special Report, *Horizon*, No 8, August, Residential Care Association, Surbiton.

RCA (1984) The Keyworker Reviewed: A Working Paper, *Horizon*, No 16 September, Residential Care Association, Surbiton.

Redding D (1991) The Key to Success, Inside the NHS and the Community Care Act, *Community Care*, 28-3, Wallington (p vi).

Renshaw J, Hampson R, Thomason C, Darton R, Judge K & Knapp M (1988) *Care in The Community: The First Steps,* Gower, Aldershot.

Riordan J, Bramhall B & Backhouse T (1988) Teamwork to Serve the Elderly, *Health Service Journal*, 19-5, London (pp 564-566).

Rivlin M (1983) Reacting to Power, *Social Work Today*, 2-8, Birmingham (p 21).

Rodway S (1979) The Concept of the Keyworker: Is it "Pie and the Sky"? An Employer's Viewpoint, *Social Work Service*, 19-3, Department of Health and Social Security, London (pp 45-47).

Ross S & Bilson A (1989) *Social Work Management and Practice: Systems Principles*, Jessica Kingsley, London.

Sackville A (1979) The Concept of the Keyworker: A Challenge to Traditional Thinking, *Social Work Service,* 19-3, Department of Health and Social Security, London (pp 40-44).

Savage A (1985) Quoted in Challis D, Darton R, Johnson L & Stone M (1988) Multi-Skilled Carers in the Community, *Social Work Today*, 4-8, London (pp 13-15).

SCA (1988) *The Social Care Task*, Social Care Association, Surbiton.

SCA (1990) *Action Check List for Anti-Racist Practice in Social Care,* Social Care Association, Surbiton.

SCA (1991) *Keyworking in Social Care, An Introductory Guide*, Social Care Association, Surbiton.

SCA (1993) *The Social Care Task: Improving the Quality of Life*, Social Care Association, Surbiton.

SCA/BASW (1987) *Review and Prospect: 10 Years of Keyworking*, Unpublished Report, Social Care Association, Surbiton.

Seebohm Report (1968) *Report of The Committee On Local Authority and Allied Social Services,* HMSO, London.

Senior B (1989) Residential Care: What Hope for the Future? in Langan & Lee (above)

Siddiqui S (1991) Ways to Shelter from the Strain, *Care Weekly*, 19-4, pp 10-11.

Sills P (1988) The Learning Curve, *Care Weekly*, 12-8 (p 10).

SSI (1989) *Doing it Better Together, A Report of Developments in Four Locations to Establish Local Procedures for Multidisciplinary Assessment of the Needs of Elderly People*, Social Services Inspectorate, Department of Health, London.

Sutton C (1979) *Psychology for Social Workers and Counsellors: An Introduction*, Routledge and Kegan Paul, London.

Tavener P (1989) Ideas in Action: Supervision and The Nature of The Organisation, *Social Work Education*, Vol. 8 No 2, Spring (pp 25-28).

Taylor J (1985) Meresworth, Home Within a Home in McDerment L & Greengross S (Eds) *Social Care for Elderly People,* An International Perspective, Social Care Association, Surbiton.

Tossell D & Webb R (1986) *Inside the Caring Services*, Edward Arnold, London.

Townsend P (1962) *The Last Refuge*, Routledge & Kegan Paul, London.

Truax CB & Carkhuff RR (1967) *Towards Effective Counselling and Psychotherapy*, Aldine, Chicago.

Unwin H (1987) Some Research Concerning General Management Skills in Sutton C (Ed) *A Handbook of Research for the Helping Professions*, Routledge and Kegan Paul, London.

Vernon J & Fruin D (1986) *In Care: A Study of Social Work Decision Making*, National Children's Bureau, London.

Ward L (1978) The Keyworker Concept, *Social Work Today*, 13-6, Birmingham (p 1).

Wendelken C (1983) *Children In and Out of Care*, Heinemann Educational, London.

Westheimer IJ (1977) *The Practice of Supervision in Social Work, A Guide for Supervisors,* Ward Lock Educational, London.
White KJ (1979) United Kingdom: Independent Long Stay Children's Home in Payne C & White K (Eds) *Caring for Deprived Children,* Croom Helm, London.
Woodcock M (1979) *Team Development Manual,* Gower, Aldershot.
Woolrych R (1987) Is Management the Answer to Problems Facing CHMTs? *Social Work Today,* 7-9, London.
Younghusband E (1978) *Social Work in Britain: 1950-1975,* George Allen & Unwin, London.